THE EYES HAVE IT

The Eyes Have It

How to Market in an Age of
Divergent Consumers, Media Chaos
and Advertising Anarchy

*

Kevin Lee

with Steve Baldwin

EASTON STUDIO PRESS · 2007

Books are available at special discounts when purchased in bulk for premiums and sales promotions, as well as for fund-raising or educational uses. Special editions or book excerpts can be created to customer specifications. For details and further information, contact:

Special Sales Director
Easton Studio Press
P.O. Box 3131
Westport, CT 06883
(203) 454-4454

www.eastonsp.com

Contact the authors at kevin.lee@didit.com and steve.baldwin@didit.com

Printed in the United States of America

First Printing: September 2007
10 9 8 7 6 5 4 3 2 1

Book design & composition by Mark McGarry, Texas Type & Book Works
Set in Minion

*To all my clients who continue to ask the hard questions,
pushing me to guide them through the increasingly complex
marketing landscape so that they might transform
their companies to thrive under the
new advertising ecosystem.*

Contents

Foreword: Joanne Bradford, Corporate Vice President,
Chief Media Officer, MSN   XI

Introduction: The Transformation of the Advertising
and Media Ecosystem   XIII

1   **Eye of the Storm: Madison Avenue in Crisis**   1

    1.1   An Empire Built on Image, Imprecision, and Waste   2

    1.2   The Dawn of Media Targeting   5

    1.3   The Dawn of Interactivity   7

    1.4   From Prime Time to My Time   14

    1.5   Evidence of Untargeted Media's Declining Effectiveness   17

    1.6   Why Ad Agencies Are Paralyzed   23

    1.7   Other Sources of Madison Avenue's Denial   25

    1.8   Why Even Great Industries Fail to Adjust to Disruptive Change   27

    1.9   Solutions for Marketers: Can You Trust Your Ad Agency?   29

    1.10   Solutions for Agencies: Be an Agent of Reform at Your Agency   31

2   **Eyestrain: Digital Marketing Isn't Easy**
(And It Isn't Going to Get Easier)   33

    2.1   Digital Marketing Grows Up   34

    2.2   The Rise of Search   36

    2.3   Search Engines Morph into Media Exchanges   46

    2.4   Increased Power, Increased Complexity   49

    2.5   Solutions: Get Help from a Best-of-Breed Agency   58

2.6   Solutions: Build Your Organization's Search Competency   62

2.7   Solutions: Successful Digital Marketing Means Investing
      in Data   66

3   Eyes Wide Shut: The Media Plan Is Obsolete   69

3.1   Digital Media is Hard to Plan For   69

3.2   New Methods of Valuing Advertising   72

3.3   From Silo'd to Integrated Marketing   74

3.4   From Manual to Automated Media Exchanges   76

3.5   Erosion of "Upfront" Media Buying   80

3.6   Will Marketers Actually Buy Media This Way?   83

3.7   Solutions: Build a Media Slush Fund   87

3.8   Solutions: Build a Nimble Team   89

3.9   Solutions: Don't Fall in Love with Your Media Plan   91

4   Lyin' Eyes: The New Search Engine and Digital Media
    Marketplaces are Neither Fair nor Transparent   93

4.1   What the Search Engines Won't Tell You   94

4.2   Your Money Isn't Good Enough   96

4.3   Do Search Engines Have a Bias Against Segmentation?   99

4.4   Warning: the Search Marketplace Is Not a Mall   102

4.5   A Search Engine Tax?   103

4.6   The Click Fraud Conundrum   107

4.7   The SEO Trap   113

4.8   Solutions: Adjust to the New Unknowables   115

5   20:20 Vision: Branding Is Not Dead   117

5.1   How Digital Marketing Redefines the Branding Process   118

5.2   Why Brand Marketers Are Confused   120

5.3   Why Brands Have an Advantage Online   122

5.4   Quantifying the Brand Advantage   124

5.5   Brand Lift and Search Marketing   125

5.6 Brand Opportunities in Keywords 126

5.7 Solutions: Think Holistically, but Act Practically 129

5.8 Solutions: Model Branding Interaction Effects 130

5.9 Solutions: Use BEI and Site Engagement as Proxies
for Measuring Branding Effectiveness 131

5.10 Solutions: Practice Defensive Branding 134

6 Eye of the Robot: Technology Is Central (But It Isn't Enough) 137

6.1 Basic Digital Marketing Issues 138

6.2 Advanced Digital Marketing Issues 141

6.3 Solutions: Build a Tech-Savvy Team 143

7 Fleeting Eyes: Change Is the Only Constant 149

7.1 Perils of Marketing to Fickle Audiences 149

7.2 Organic Search Results: An Endangered Species? 152

7.3 The PC-Browser-SERP Paradigm Is Not Immutable 155

7.4 New Digital Marketing Channels Will Have Different
Marketing Potentials 157

7.5 Digital Marketing: Too Powerful to Be Left Alone? 159

7.6 Solutions: Guard Your Data 162

7.7 Solutions: You Need a Translator 163

7.8 Solutions: If You Can't Do This Work In-House
Outsource It 164

8 Eyes on the Prize: Assessing the Digital Marketing
Opportunities Provided by Today's Major Players 169

8.1 Google 170

8.2 Yahoo 173

8.3 Microsoft 175

8.4 Other Players to Watch 178

9 Conclusions 185

Foreword

It's a very exciting time to be working in online media. The opportunity that people have to connect to people and information they care about is unprecedented. There are many keys to success in digital marketing, but the most fundamental is an understanding of the consumer. At Microsoft we've built a very successful software business from understanding the crossroads of consumers and technology. Now we are bringing these insights to marketers who need to understand how advertising can stand inside that same intersection.

Amidst all of this change, we are learning that the mode of communication matters less and less to more and more people. As marketers, we need to focus less on what application or device our customers is using and instead focus on how we can facilitate connections among people and the information they care about most. Understanding how we can satisfy these core human needs should come first. Figuring out how the technology enables this should follow.

Advances in technology have allowed marketers and publishers to be more accountable than ever before for the experiences consumers have with their brands. We have to ensure that our research and measurement techniques are keeping pace with the innovations in the media landscape. We know that for many marketers the risks of experimentation in interactive advertising will remain an obstacle until we have reliable measurement mechanisms in place to judge successes and failures.

In this context, marketers and publishers need to think not just about to reach our consumers, but how to engage them. We have to think very creatively about how we define experiences that engage consumers' emotion and attention.

Consumers have moved out from our old models and are interacting in a way that media and marketers have never seen before. They're communicating and getting information faster than ever before. Their media behavior has evolved with technology... now we as marketers have to catch up with them. It's a playground of opportunity.

JOANNE K. BRADFORD
Corporate Vice President, Chief Media Officer, MSN

Introduction

The Transformation of the Advertising and Media Ecosystem

"I believe today's marketing model is broken. We're applying antiquated thinking and work systems to a new world of possibilities."

—Jim Stengel, P&G CMO

*

THE CURRENT STATE of advertising—the way media is bought, the way inventory is sold, and the way ad messages are delivered to consumers—is dying a slow but steady death. Media buyers at the big agencies—despite the increasing ability to target campaigns—instead opt for tonnage, blasting out advertising that is neither relevant nor interesting to the vast majority of consumers. Although there are many factors driving the death of traditional advertising, there is a glimmer of hope. This hope comes in the form of enhanced targeting. Super-niche targeting has the ability to deliver what is nearly unheard of in mainstream advertising: relevance. When responsive and willing consumers notice ad messages, engage with Web content, and interact with brands within an advertiser's web site, that's the Holy Grail of marketing.

From about 1950 to around 1980, the eyes of most Americans focused on a glowing TV screen tuned to a small handful of possible channels. The reason there were so few channels available was due to a fact of physics: the FCC, working with a limited number of viable VHF frequencies in the electromagnetic spectrum, had allocated thirteen for use by broadcasters (Channels 1 through 13 with Channel 1 reserved for low-power community stations). The VHF channels 2 through 13 were the high-power stations and were used to carry commercial broadcasting programs.

This inherent limitation of high-power VHF licenses, however, made the work of marketers amazingly easy. If an advertiser wanted to get his message out to the multitudes, the marketer simply called up his ad agency, which then concocted an arresting thirty-second spot and ran it during a top-rated show on the big three networks: ABC, CBS, or NBC. The result was a marketing message that half of the American population in 1950 would see. Over the years, as the penetration of TV into U.S. households grew, the diversity of broadcast channels did not, and by 1955 the penetration rate was 85 percent. The target—the aggregated eyeballs of millions—was so big that it was difficult to miss.

One commentator has called this media environment the "saturation bombing" era of advertising. Get enough bombers in the air over an enemy city, open the bomb bay doors, and you'd destroy enough of your target to justify saying that you'd completed your mission. Instead of dropping bombs, of course, advertisers ran commercials, their favorite weapon being the thirty-second spot. And for decades this approach worked just fine because ad agencies and media firms knew exactly where America's eyes were (in living rooms), what they were doing (staring passively at the glowing screen from their Barcaloungers), and what they were watching (the three networks and their affiliates). For years TV was so new and novel that both the content and advertising was consumed with equal enthusiasm. Then the addition of color to television created a second wave of novelty.

Mass broadcasting had two amazing assets: its tremendous reach, and its richness, which allowed ad men to spin elaborate dreams about how to achieve happiness, fulfillment, and social status through the purchase of a given product. Creativity—not media targeting—was the coin of the realm in this dream process; it was the unique differentiator that determined whether a given consumer bought brand A instead of brand B. Because of this, advertising agencies prided themselves on hiring the best, the brightest, and most creative people they could find. As all advertisers played by the same simple rules, the main focus of the ad industry was to innovate the content of advertising, not how it was served. Good ads—ads that made you remember and feel fondly about a given product or brand—were gold. Bad ads, which did none of these things, would sooner or later get the responsible ad agency canned. Because the media model was so simple, Madison Avenue's main asset was its creative talent: the folks whose "big ideas" and bold imaginative leaps gave fire to ad campaigns. Visionary stars such as David Ogilvy, Leo Burnett, Raymond Rubicom, and Bill Bernbach led innovative shops known for their ability to style unique messages that stuck in America's mind. The creative directors that worked under them were responsible for spinning the dreams, and 90 percent of the collective mental effort on Madison Avenue was funneled into the message, not the medium that would carry it.

The media planning department, on the other hand, was the site where the mechanics of dream-spinning met the realities of actually buying the air time and evaluating the effectiveness of the spent ad dollar. During the early years of broadcast and print media, in the agency organization hierarchy, these dingy departments were one step up from the mail room. They were backwaters where young recruits, fresh out of school, endured the process of learning the basics of media buying: how to understand a magazine rate sheet, what acronyms such as CPM and GRP meant, how to audit where and when a given ad ran, and other mundane tasks. The obviousness of the media plan due to the dearth of options and the limited permutations of broadcast and print media stifled any real creativity in the media department. Even if a media person came up with an innovative way to reach the advertiser's demographic less expensively or more effectively, chances are no one was paying attention. Anyone with any real talent and ambition didn't stay long in media planning because the real action was way upstairs in the account management and creative departments, where the real gods of Madison Avenue cooked up their big ideas, schmoozed with reps from GM, Kellogg's, and Kraft over three-martini lunches, and played cards together in the New Haven Railroad bar car on the way back to Westport each night. In recent years, however, the advent of digital media has necessitated the requirement of an entirely new way of thinking about advertising that is as attentive to the media carrying the message as the message itself. The mass audience that was once so easy to hit in the analog era has spread into an almost infinite field of niches, and the old, assembly-line method of creating ads and beaming them to this mass of gazing eyes is quickly falling by the wayside. The media world is fast evolving from untargeted "dumb" analog media to "smart" digital media that provides transparency, accountability, and micro-targeting.

Advertising conceived and produced in the old way, in large chunks (a hundred thousand dollars spent to create a sexy commercial and a million dollars to run it across the networks) is being disaggregated. In the era of fragmentation, where media consumers are so elusive and often even resistant to nontargeted ad messages, the new approach is what has been termed "mass customization": the ability to think of advertising as a range of potential messages being sent across possible channels and presented to the consumer at the exact place and time at which he or she will be most amenable to the marketer's pitch. The old ways of "Reach and Frequency" used for gauging the power of advertising are growing less and less applicable to this new world of media, in which relevancy is now the governing value. Advertising is no longer the act of just blasting out your message to bombard enough consumers until you probably hit some of the right ones. Rather, increasingly advertising must be the right message at the right time to the right consumer through the right channel.

This new media world provides unparalleled promise, as well as unparalleled pitfalls into which the unwary marketer can fall. Our intention in this book is to illustrate the promise and the perils, and to show you how you can best exploit this new medium to the best advantage of your organization, your clients, or yourself.

Who are we and what gives us the right to have these opinions? Well, we've spent the last ten years in that off-the-radar space called search marketing. In the process we've learned our share of lessons and taken our share of hits, bought hundreds of millions of dollars, worth of media through the search engines, and watched those search engines grow from tiny little utilities without a revenue plan to corporate giants with market caps above $100 billion. We've followed Google, Yahoo, Microsoft, and others from the get-go. We've seen digital marketing grow from a relatively untargeted, tonnage-oriented industry to one that is laser-targeted and providing an unparalleled degree of control for marketers, and also developing into what is now a multibillion-dollar industry. We've witnessed data confirming that consumers engage in and are influenced by advertising in direct proportion to the targeting and relevance of that advertising. We've also seen an entirely new standard by which the effectiveness of advertising is judged, and the currency of this new realm is influence, which is now driven by relevancy and superior targeting.

What follows is a discussion of where we think the next generation of advertising is going, the issues you as a marketer will face, and how you can profit from using the new set of methods—some of them entirely new—in order to run more efficient digital marketing campaigns. This is NOT a book on Internet marketing: digital marketing campaigns are no longer confined to the Internet. If you're doing any kind of digital marketing, our hope is that you will benefit from the concepts, strategies, and insights we share in the following chapters.

CHAPTER 1

Eye of the Storm
Madison Avenue in Crisis

"Why is it package-goods manufacturers still spend only two or three percent of their ad budgets on the Net? Seventy to eighty percent of car-buying decisions are influenced by the Internet, but it's only five to ten percent of car manufacturers' budgets."

—WPP's Sir Martin Sorrell, speaking at The Digital Media Revolution conference, as reported in BusinessWeek.com, 11/9/06, http://www.businessweek.com/innovate/ FineOnMedia/archives/2006/11/scenes_from_an.html

*

A "PERFECT STORM" occurs when several different phenomena, none in themselves catastrophic, occurring at the same time and place interact, creating synergies that generate a situation much more dangerous than would be obtained from their simple additive effect. The institution of Madison Avenue, which grew to maturity in the era of mass media, finds itself in such a perfect storm today, imperiled by powerful evolutionary forces that erode its profit base and threaten to render it obsolete. These include the fragmentation of media and the empowerment of consumers over media choices, as well as increasing demands from marketers to make media buying and selling transparent and accountable. Madison Avenue's attempts to address these threats have been defensive, ineffective, and characteristic of other doomed industries challenged by disruptive forces. To answer why this happened, one must look back at how this institution evolved, and how it then failed to respond to the forces that challenged it.

1.1 An Empire Built on Image, Imprecision, and Waste

In its heyday, working in the power centers of Madison Avenue was cool and sexy, and it's no accident that Alfred Hitchcock chose an ad man as his protagonist in his classic film *North By Northwest*, or that the protagonist of the hit TV series *Bewitched* was married to an ad man. Because they spun the immortal dreams and created the iconic characters that still haunt the dreams of many—including the Jolly Green Giant, Tony the Tiger, The Marlboro Man, Mr. Whipple, Rosie the Plumber, the White Tornado, and others—ad men were at the center of mass culture.

It's no wonder that many ad men feel nostalgic for this bygone era, because for them it really was a Golden Age.

Of course, if one looks at this era through a marketer's perspective, it's more likely to be regarded as the Golden Age of the Rip Off. Because the level of accountability was nearly nonexistent, this was a time when billions of dollars changed hands without anyone really knowing whether all the millions spent by advertisers were doing anything more than making the salesmen at ABC, CBS, and NBC happy. Advertisers knew from speaking to customers that those customers remembered the advertising, and in general there was a measurable correlation between increased advertising and sales. The most highly evolved technology that Madison Avenue offered to marketers for broadcast listernership and viewership was based upon sample-based measurement methods established in the early days of commercial radio. Print circulation auditing evolved in a similar fashion with the Audit Bureau of Circulation (or ABC). Media consumption has never been precise, and it lacks the resolution required to even establish whether a given commercial or ad was seen and noticed by a consumer. Within the world of broadcast TV, data sent from Nielsen's meters, sent at fifteen-minute intervals, does not account for channel-switching (which during the early days of media measurement, before the remote control, required someone walking over to the TV and turning the knob), nor does it have the ability to know whether an individual is even in the room while a given commercial is aired. Additionally, Nielsen's reliance on viewer diaries to supplement the data supplied by its meters doesn't account for an obvious fact about people: they may not tell the truth about the programs they watched.

In the past few years, Nielsen has been under pressure to upgrade its system in order to provide minute-by-minute monitoring capabilities, but so far it has failed to provide any more than an ongoing assurance that it will do so—and the deadlines for completing this upgrade continue to be pushed further into the future. (I agree with the conspiracy theorists when they postulate that no one in the advertising and media industries wants to know the truth about TV ratings and consumer TV-watching behavior. Even CMOs who have been approving annual media plans that look disturbingly like those of years past may not want to face reality because the alternative is a complete fresh start and a ton of work for the entire corporate marketing team.)

Everybody knew that the old system was imprecise and that the "saturation bombing" era of advertising was wasteful, although nobody could really quantify how many dollars were being spent ineffectively. But some idea of the vast scope of this waste was recently brought to light by advertising research mavens Rex Briggs and Greg Stuart who, in 2006, wrote a book called *What Sticks: Why Most Advertising Fails and How to Guarantee Yours Succeeds*. Using data compiled over a five-year period and vetted by the Advertiser Research Foundation, the authors used a sample set of thirty major marketers and tracked how they bought more than a billion dollars of media, and then measured the results of such spending. Their conclusions: 37 percent of the approximately $230 billion total advertising dollars annually are wasted, amounting to some $85 billion of waste per year.

$85 billion is a lot of money, such a large sum that it's almost an abstraction. To make it a little more concrete, $85 billion is equivalent to:

1. The initial estimate made by the Congressional Budget Office for the U.S. Defense Department's 2006 needs.
2. The entire world investment in ethanol plants for the next fifteen years.
3. Enough money to buy coffee and a bagel (with cream cheese) for every adult in New York City (6 million people) each morning for twenty years. (http://www.insurancefraud.org/80_billion.htm)

Briggs and Stuart blame a number of factors for this colossal waste. For example, in far too many cases critical decisions made by CMOs and ad agencies are still being made "by gut." This approach, which eschews metrics in favor of intuition, may have worked in the 1980s when the attention of most of America could be summoned with a thirty-second spot placed on popular shows on the three major networks, but it's poison in today's diffracted media environment. Additionally, sample-based audience research is inadequate or ignored, and far too many marketers continue to use antiquated "silo" thinking that fails to bring all of the essential organizational stakeholders (sales, marketing, top management) into the ad decision-making loop.

Although Briggs and Stuart don't lay the blame for this waste exclusively on the heads of broadcasters, their findings suggest that reform, when it comes, will come from outside the advertising establishment. After all—that wasted $85 billion might not be doing a thing for marketers, but it's being pocketed by those who run media. From the broadcasters' perspective, the lost money isn't waste: it's profit, so there is zero incentive for media owners to fix the system. And the agencies would put themselves out of business if they cut media budgets by 37 percent or more.

Why did advertisers tolerate this enormous level of waste? Quite simply, in the analog era there existed no less wasteful way of reaching large masses of people. You had to buy tonnage, which is still relied upon by the media plans of the top one hundred advertising spenders. But in today's world this calculus no longer need apply. There are choices for consumers, choices for marketers, and methods that can eliminate much of the waste that once was an unavoidable price associated with buying media.

1.2 The Dawn of Media Targeting

The idea that there might be a much less wasteful way of doing advertising evolved in the 1950s, first taking root not in the world of broadcasting but in print. While GM or Kellogg's were perfectly happy dropping tons of money into broadcasting, because cars and corn flakes were products that just about every American could be expected to one day buy, there were plenty of marketers who didn't want to buy advertising by the ton—or sell products by the ton.

To cater to these marketers, who tended to be thriftier with their marketing dollars than CPG (Consumer Packaged Goods) giants seeking to move tons of diapers or tons of toothpaste, the special interest publishing industry was born, offering advertisers an alternative to placing ads in untargeted electronic media or in general interest magazines such as *Life* and *Look* that offered large but undifferentiated audiences. Buying ad positioning in one of these magazines was appropriate for manufacturers of more general products, such as automobiles, soap, soup, shoes, whiskey, and cigarettes, but not for manufacturers of more specialized products. The vast majority of people viewing these advertisements were not interested in such specialized products, so for those manufacturers such media would be a waste of ad dollars.

The movement toward a more segmented media model was led by magazine publishing entrepreneurs such as William B. Ziff, who in the early 1950s launched specialized magazines such as *Modern Boating*, *Flying*, and *Car and Driver*. Ziff was among the first to notice one of the most retrospectively obvious features of life in postwar America: that leisure time was expanding and many Americans, as inherently action- and activity-oriented people, were constantly searching for ways to fill this new time that was becoming increasingly available because of advances in technologies. *Modern Boating* was launched to cater to the large segment of returning World War II and Korean War sailors who wanted to convert their former profession into a hobby; *Flying* targeted returning aviators who had been bitten by the flying bug, and *Car and Driver* catered to the many Americans whose passion for the automobile extended far beyond their sojourn in the driver's seat. These magazines all worked according to a carefully crafted formula. By providing extensive product reviews, they helped their readers to make educated decisions about products they were already in the market to buy. By providing a segmented, passionate audience to advertisers, specialized magazines provided more bang for the advertising buck than could ever be delivered by a general-interest magazine.

These targeted publications were amazingly profitable. As it turned out, advertisers were willing to pay as much to reach a smaller group of people who were more likely to actually act on their marketing messages than a larger group of undifferentiated viewers. In fact, some were willing to pay much more, and Ziff quickly built an empire of publications based upon the simple realization that by identifying a niche audience through the creation of something of specific interest to them, advertisers seeking the attention of these consumers would flock to these magazines in droves. Even though the circulations of these niche publications were a small fraction of the general interest magazines, the CPM (Cost Per Thousand readers) could be significantly higher. Additionally, Ziff discovered another interesting thing about the way advertising works in targeted media channels: instead of being repelled by it, consumers actually seemed to like it. Readers of *Modern Boating* didn't mind being exposed to commercial messages touting a new Evinrude outboard engine that provided 25 percent more horsepower. In fact, they welcomed this information, not only because it was information they might use in a future purchase, but also because it increased their community status. When one of their old navy buddies called and asked them about what outboard motor to buy, the *Modern Boating* reader could draw upon the information in the ad they'd seen. Advertising, if it became *relevant,* wasn't perceived as advertising anymore: it was simply *information,* and useful information to boot. Furthermore, the question about advertising effectiveness evolved from "*how many people saw my ad?*" to "*how many people who actually are in-market or have a high chance of being in-market in the future saw my ad?*" And the idea of advertising relevance continues to be a central theme in the ongoing evolution of advertising.

1.3 The Dawn of Interactivity

Electronic advertising was historically a "push medium" that piggy-backed itself on one-way, synchronous channels providing little or no interactive possibilities. But in the early 1990s, thanks to the widespread proliferation of personal computers and the advent of early dial-up networks, what had been a broad one-way channel boulevard started to become a multitude of two-way streets. Within that decade, the world saw the dawn of interactive networks such as CompuServe, Prodigy, and AOL, the birth of the World Wide Web, the invention of the DVR, and the forerunners to time-shifting media devices such as the iPod.

Although early online systems were slow, crude, and clunky, they had one distinctive characteristic that made them so radically unlike prior media technologies that its importance continues to be understated. They were what engineers call "full-duplex" systems, which allowed for the exchange of data both up and downstream. This bidirectional quality was more akin to telephones and telegraphs than radio, TV, or other one-way, one-to-many communications systems.

Besides being slow, the early online services used proprietary architectures that were not interoperable. However, as each online service was pressed by its usership to increasingly open its doors to the vast reaches of content available on the Internet, all this would change. As a result, more traffic began to flow across standardized TCP/IP networks, which happen to have a revolutionary property: unlike analog media, they have intelligence built into them. Packets, unlike broadcast signals, are constructed in a way that is essentially self-aware: they know who sent them, who their intended recipient is, and where they are going. In essence, digital media have accountability built into their very core. This is why all digital media are inherently smarter than the old broadcast models, and also why they have the potential of providing so much more insight—transparency—into the effectiveness of advertising carried across them.

For a long time, because users of these early systems tended to be hobbyists, geeks, and academics, the increasing use of digital communications systems in order to bypass established media structures was regarded as more of a curiosity than the beginning of an authentic media revolution. In the early 1990s, the number of people using networked personal computers was vastly smaller than the numbers watching television, which made it easy for Madison Avenue to dismiss digital media as a technological fad that would pass, much like the CB radio craze of the 1970s.

But when the World Wide Web came along in 1994, providing a

truly interactive and multimedia experience for the masses, the flood-
gates broke open. Suddenly anyone, anywhere, with an Internet connection and less than an hour of training could cobble together a web
page with some text, upload a picture or two, and experience the thrill
of linking to and being linked from someone else's page anywhere in
the world. Although few consumers took advantage of the power to
self-publish in the early days of the Internet, within just a couple years
there were enough web pages to keep consumers with either niche or
general interests occupied and engaged. E-mail quickly became a killer
app, and despite the proliferation of spam(unsolicited commercial
e-mail messages), e-mail continues to be a core element of the
Internet.

The insurgent spirit of the nascent medium was aptly captured by
colorful visionaries such as John Perry Barlow, who in 1996 wrote the
"Declaration of Independence for Cyberspace," an audacious document declaring that the Web consisted of a completely new society with
its own morays, rules, and spirit that would bow neither to the time-
worn rules of the media establishment or the will of duly authorized
regularity bodies. Barlow's document was widely circulated, bracing
the Web's early adopters with its outlaw spirit.

Futurist firebrands were joined by forward-thinking marketers and
site publishers who invented the first ad banners, which were embedded within web pages provided by popular content portals of the era,
including Wired.com, Lycos, and Time-Warner's Pathfinder. These ad
banners were sold in a way familiar to media buyers of broadcast and
print media: by the impression, reckoned in CPM. Marketers bought
these impressions by lot (e.g., 35,000 impressions at X CPM), and they
were rotated through the portal sites either in a completely untargeted
way (i.e., RON or Run of Network) or across "channels" (another term
borrowed from television), which provided a more targeted audience
more likely to act upon the call to action of the banner. Premium posi-

tions (such as a placement on a home page or high-traffic area) were paid for by "slotting fees."

Ad banners remained the dominant form of Web-based marketing for almost ten years, and the means by which they are served has remained, for the most part, untargeted. Like roadside billboards, their prominent position on portal sites guaranteed that just about everybody passing through a portal would see them, some fraction would click on them, and some smaller fraction of these clickers would actually heed the marketer's call to action. Today, they are still widely used by brand marketers who are not bothered by the idea that for most people the banners are irrelevant and most of the impressions they pay for are wasted. These marketers are less interested in the targeting possibilities of the Internet than the fact that, compared to other forms of media, it remains dirt cheap. For them, it's all just a numbers game. If you can get your message out in front of millions of eyeballs, and get a certain share of them to click on your ad, and a subset of those to actually answer your call to action, it's worth laying out plenty of cash

Early Ad Banners Running Across Time-Warner's Pathfinder Network (1995–1998)

(Yahoo rents out the prime position on its home page on a daily basis for $500,000 per day).

In retrospect, looking back at the dawn of the Web and thinking about how marketers initially thought about it, it's amazing how much they seemed to regard it as a mere extension of predigital media. This fixation with media's past—the world of the billboard, the interruptive thirty-second spot, and the daily, periodically delivered newspaper— actually spawned an entire subindustry of "push media" companies such as Pointcast, iFusion, and Marimba, as each sought to convert the two-way functionality of the Web into a passive, info-pushing channel. On Pointcast's web site, it proclaimed that it had found a way to eliminate the need for people to hunt for information. Ironically the con-

Untargeted Banner Ad (Ford) Running Across Prominent
Areas of Yahoo's Home Page in 2006

cept of push media is returning, this time on an open standard of RSS (Real Simple Syndication) and intelligent agents. A similarly powerful misunderstanding of the medium occurred when large media companies launched "portals," areas whose content was so "sticky" that the user would never need to venture out of these "walled gardens" to the ugly and dangerous world that lay beyond it.

In the late 1990s there were many missteps, misconceptions, and Internet business models that, with the benefit of hindsight, look completely half-baked. For a while it seemed that everybody in America was running a portal, or an e-commerce company, or a community site, or a Web design company, or had money invested in an Internet company. As long as speculative fever reigned supreme on Wall Street, there was no limit in a media with no real rules. Of course, when Wall Street ran out of patience, all of this crashed, and by 2001 most of these experiments lay in ruins with their owners bankrupt, living back at their parents' houses, or living in their cars.

Despite the crazy schemes, lost billions, bruised egos, and widespread misperception among old media professionals that the Internet was merely a cheap distribution channel for prior media forms, the Internet survived the dot-com craze. And despite the hype in the business press that "the Web is dead," with every passing month the Internet is becoming more deeply established in the lives of those who seek to partake of its astonishing treasure of riches. It has taken a long time for "pull media"—media invoked by the user—to gather steam again, but it did so with the rise of search engines, which in the later portion of the 1990s began to morph from hard-to-use, ugly, and clunky engines into elegant information machines that satisfied demand.

We will discuss the way the advertising ecosystem has been revolutionized by search engines in Chapter 3. For now, let us observe that search engine marketing represents a complete change in the way advertising is accomplished and is the most important driver of the recent growth of digital marketing as an alternative method available to marketers to help them accomplish their strategic business objectives.

The advent of search engines revitalized and redefined the way advertising was created, distributed, and paid for, subsequently opening up a new world of precise targeting, accountability, and transparency for the digital marketer. Today, Google, Yahoo, and Microsoft are the "big three" engines commanding the majority of search query traffic, and Google is by far the strongest of the three, handling almost half of the searches conducted.

Although search marketing is not the only effective digital marketing method, it is the driver of online advertising growth and, in the American Advertising Federation's 2006 Survey of Industry Leaders on

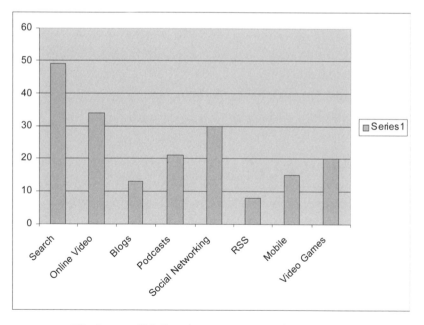

Effectiveness of Medium (average percentages). Source: AAF

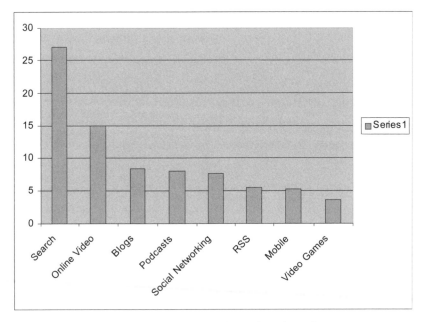

Percentage of Online Media Budget Planned
to Allocate in 2007 (average percentages). Source: AAF

Advertising Industry and New Media Trends, was deemed the "most effective" new media option.

Consequently, search marketing is increasingly perceived by marketers as a means of getting more for their advertising dollar.

1.4 From Prime Time to My Time

Analog electronic media was and is what is termed "appointment based." If you couldn't arrange to be in front of a TV when *Gunsmoke* or *Dragnet* was on, you missed out. Like an unwanted guest, advertising interrupted these appointments and was deliberately inserted in ways that maximized the impact of this intrusion, often by using audio compression to annoyingly boost its audio volume levels above that of the programming surrounding it. In fact, advertising informed

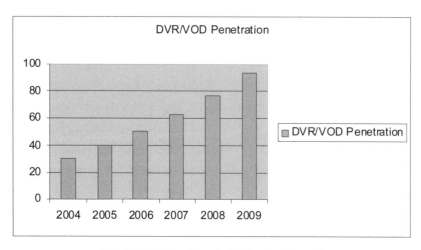

U.S. Digital Video Recorder/Video On Demand
Penetration (in millions). Source: Forrester Research
to Allocate in 2007 (average percentages). Source: AAF

the structure of entertainment intimately: television programming
was even deliberately scripted to provide "cliffhangers" designed to
keep users in place during the commercials so that they would not
miss the first minute of the programming once it resumed. First-run
movies appearing on television had crucial scenes removed to provide
enough time for commercials to fit into the allocated 90- or 120-
minute time slot. Schedules were painstakingly assembled like puzzle
pieces in order to maximize broadcaster's maximum "lead in" and
"lead out" advantages.

The VCR, which began appearing en masse in American households in the early 1980s, was the first widely accepted time-shifting
device. Although its success led to the explosion of the home video
market in successive years, its time-shifting capabilities were limited
and not widely adapted, a fact empirically obvious to observers noting
that the internal clocks of these machines were rarely advanced past
"12:00 midnight." The next generation of time-shifting devices, however, was easier to program and was equipped with features specifically

designed to zap commercials, which came in predictable thirty-second segments.

Users flocked to time-shifting devices such as TiVo and those offered by cable companies not only because they wanted to watch shows they missed. By far the most popular feature of these devices was their ability to zap commercials, and between 65 and 75 percent of them did so regularly (J. D. Power and Associates study, 2004).

It's no wonder that the ad-zapping features of TiVo were so popular. Commercial television viewers, who had for years abided by free TV's basic social contract that called for the endurance of commercials in exchange for "free" entertainment, gradually realized that broadcast networks were abusing their side of the bargain by loading up each hour of air time with as many commercials as possible. In fact, according to a study by PhaseOne consultants, by 2003 one hour in four consisted completely of commercials, on-air promotional spots, and public service announcements (reported in Broadcasting and Cable, 12/22/03, http://www.reedtelevision.com/article/CA359499.html?display=TV+Buyer).

TiVo and other time-shifting technologies were the first real instance of consumers reaching into their wallets to invest in warding off the incessant flow of commercial messages that drifted into their homes constantly via untargeted analog channels. For the first time, consumers were exercising control—and that sent shock waves through the advertising industry. Soon, as the Internet increasingly became a central force in consumers' media consumption universe, they would exercise an even greater degree of control. That initiative, plus a far wider number of possible media choices, was always inherent to the Internet, which, as it grew, became more capable of carrying more divergent forms of content aboard its intelligent packets. On it, one can watch TV, listen to the radio, and read newspaper and magazine content whenever and wherever. In effect, the Web's most power-

ful aspect is its ability to emulate a remote control device that addresses
a theoretically infinite number of channels. A remote control that
touches, or will soon touch, every piece of media ever made and can be
used to create, synthesize, zap, jam, and reprogram this media in any
way its user sees fit.

1.5 Evidence of Untargeted Media's Declining Effectiveness

Every piece of objective evidence suggests that the multiplicity of alternative, highly compelling communications channels, from the Web to
time-shifting devices such as the iPod and TiVo, is rapidly eroding the
centrality of broadcasting in America's media consumption mix. What's
amazing is how long it's taken Madison Avenue to respond to the
diminution of its historical power. Although the broadcast industry's
ability to aggregate eyeballs has been falling for almost two decades, its
response to its own declining influence, rather than adjusting rates

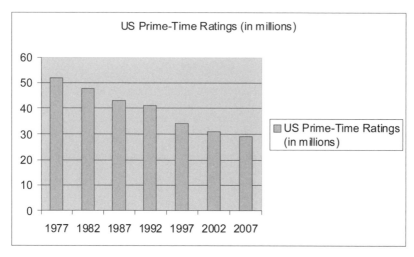

Broadcast Television's Declining Prime-Time Audience.
Source: Veronis Suhler Stevensen

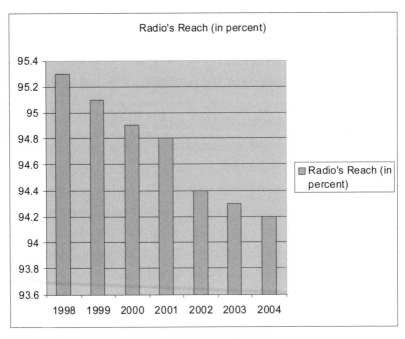

Broadcast Radio's Declining Reach Among Population Twelve and Older.
Source Arbitron: "Radio Today: How America Listens to Radio, 2005 Edition,"
December 22, 2004, reprinted in journalism.org

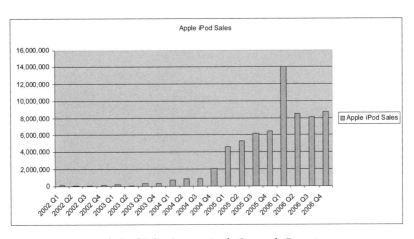

Apple iPod Sales. Source: Apple Quarterly Reports

downward to take account for the decreased value of the airtime it sells, it has consistently *upped* these rates, charging marketers more money for a less useful commodity. In fact, reaching 1,000 people on broadcast TV cost just $7.64 in 1994; by 2004 this cost had more than doubled to $19. (Mentioned in *Ad Age*, 4/21/05, "The Chaos Scenario.")

It is not possible to precisely quantify the degree to which the broadcasting industry has continued to enrich itself at the expense of marketers, but by correlating the amount of time people are spending watching television with the amount of money that the broadcasting industry is taking in can offer a rough indication. One would expect that the revenues collected by the broadcast industry would have declined as the average number of hours spent consuming broadcast media has declined. Instead, they have actually increased.

Many measurable factors contribute to the decreasing effectiveness of broadcast media. Intuitively, the increasing number of homes with

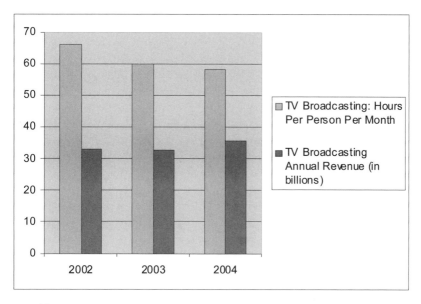

Monthly Hours Spent Consuming Broadcast Media, Correlated Against TV Broadcast Revenues, 2002–2004. Source: Statistical Abstract of the U.S., U.S. Census 2006

high-speed Internet access in addition to the increasing amount of time spent online constitute long-term secular trends that undermine television's effectiveness.

A less visible but equally significant factor is the marked degradation of the general quality of mass entertainment available on nonsubscription TV channels. Programming that people are willing to pay for, including *The Sopranos, Deadwood, Six Feet Under,* etc., is carried on paid-subscription cable channels.

On the other hand, with a declining audience, dwindling rate base, and fewer dollars to spend on quality programming, ad-supported mass broadcasting has largely found itself under siege. The result is that broadcasters are less willing to spend money creating shows that people are willing to watch, resulting in a ghetto of game shows and reality programming that few find compelling beyond the first few episodes. At the same time, the size of the average advertising "pod"

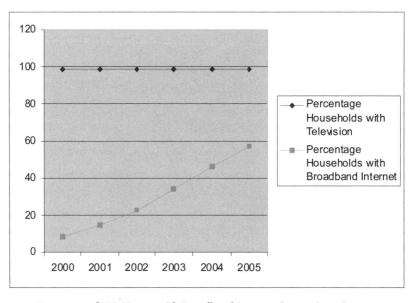

Percentage of U.S. Homes with Broadband Internet Connections. Source: Nielsen/NetRatings, U.S. Census Statistical Abstract of the United States

has expanded to the point that viewers are faced with a 25 percent chance of a commercial running at any one time when watching between 7 and 11 p.m. (TNS analysis, cited on EphronMedia.com, 12/16/06).

Even as advertisers continue to add clutter to TV programming, thereby reducing its viewability and driving increasing numbers of people to subscription channels, the quality of alternative digital programming has improved enough over the past few years to constitute a serious threat to broadcast TV's claim as a primary entertainment media. Web sites big and small contain more compelling content than ever, and as the number of broadband connections has grown, the number of people able to enjoy these "rich media" forms has expanded greatly. These Web properties also frequently contain TV-like elements, and cheap, open-source-based Web programming tools have allowed small players to produce much more professional content and communities. YouTube.com, a site that did not even exist two years ago, represents the most visible challenge to broadcast's role as the entertainment mainstay: today, YouTube receives 20 million monthly visitors, serves up 100 million video clips per day, and daily receives more than 50,000 user-generated video clips. (Nielsen/NetRatings).

The result is that the Web has begun to be appreciated as a more interesting place to consume media, and marketing dollars have begun to follow. In fact, in a survey conducted by USC-Annenberg's Digital Future Project in 2006, 43 percent of the 2,000 people polled reported that they "feel as strongly" about their online communities as they do about those in the real world.

Consequently, television advertising has become more expensive at exactly the same time that it is becoming less effective. A recent McKinsey & Co. report noted that ad spending on prime-time broadcast TV has increased over the last decade by about 40 percent even as viewers have dropped by almost 50 percent. Furthermore, the report noted that "traditional TV advertising will be one-third as effective in 2010 as it was in 1990." (*Ad Age*, 8/10/06).

Furthermore, these Census Department numbers may actually err on the conservative side. In February 2006, a JupiterResearch survey of 3,000 Internet users pegged their monthly Internet use at fifty-six hours per month, almost exactly the same amount as television. (*Media Life Magazine*, 1/1/06). According to the survey, Internet use measured by time spent dwarfs all other forms of media, including magazine reading (four hours), newspaper reading (eight hours) or radio (twenty hours).

Equally clear is that the increased amount of time spent viewing digital media is done at the expense of traditional media.

Even more strikingly, the Internet is increasingly perceived as a more important communications medium than television. In a 2006 Arbitron/Edison Media Research study that asked, "suppose from this moment on you were given the following two choices . . . either you

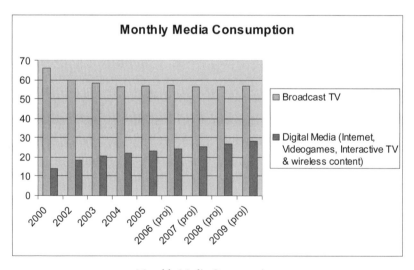

Monthly Media Consumption.
Source: Statistical Abstract of the US, U.S. Census 2006

could never watch television again OR you could never access the Internet gain," 59 percent of Americans elected never to watch television again, rather than lose access to the Internet. (Arbitron/Edison: Internet and Multimedia 2006 study).

Essentially, the media establishment's two main constituencies—the consumers who have endured its commercials and the marketers who have underwritten its programming—are rebelling, albeit for different reasons. For the first time, just as marketers have become less willing to tolerate the flaws of the old system, a credible contender to broadcast media has arrived. And yet a paltry 7 percent of U.S. total advertising spent is allocated to online media. What's wrong with this picture?

1.6 Why Ad Agencies Are Paralyzed

While the broadcast industry has been working to temporarily delay the inevitable reckoning with its declining power and influence, its tra-

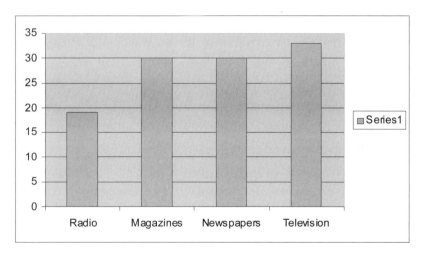

Percent of Americans Spending Less
Time with Traditional Media Due to Internet Use

ditional partners, the advertising agencies, have done little or nothing to move the basic advertising paradigm into the digital era. Advertising is still conceived as something pushed to a largely undifferentiated, captive audience in fixed temporal batches at fixed points in time followed by very limited information provided for the marketer about what good it did.

One need not look very far to find why Madison Avenue is having such difficulty thinking its way out of its current problem. Traditionally, it has made its profits through an economy-of-scale process similar the old assembly line. Take a "big idea," manufacture a limited set of (very expensive) commercial messages with it, and beam them across America using the brute force of the broadcast networks. Buy time in big blocks from the networks, mark it up, and pocket the check. By being able to reuse this limited set of assets and take advantage of market clout, economies of scale were realized, and this same asset could be used many times before its effectiveness began to burn out.

But in a media landscape fragmented into a theoretically infinite number of channels, this approach is exactly the wrong approach. Customizability, not standardization, is what is required, and creating customized messages capable of being perceived as relevant by a demassified audience is not easy. Instead of stamping out a limited number of messages at great cost and serving each identical one to a large number of recipients, the creation of a much larger number of creative elements, each targeted to an individual niche, is required. An example of this technique is used in Addressable Advertising, which calls for targeted ad insertions to be placed into programming depending upon variables about the recipient. It is also practiced in search marketing, wherein a large number of individual creative elements are associated with individual keywords or keyword combinations.

A fragmented media landscape calls for an entirely new way of regarding creative elements. In nautical terms, yesterday's thirty-second spot might be likened to a battleship, whereas today's creatives need to be small, individually targeted patrol boats. To use an analogy borrowed from computers, the existing creative paradigm is based on a WORM (write once, read many) model. But what is called for is a transformation into a WMRO (write many, read once) model, and because it is not the way they were trained to create advertising, the prospect of having to do this kind of mass customization work gives Creative Directors nightmares.

1.7 Other Sources of Madison Avenue's Denial

Some of the reasons behind Madison Avenue's failure to face the future are cultural and historical: in its glory days, "creatives" ruled the roost on Madison Avenue, and such people regarded media buyers as unimaginative number-crunchers whose sole job was to determine the mechanics that allowed their brilliant thirty-second mini-movies to reach the most people. Remember the H. G. Welles novel *The Time Machine*? In it, there was a future human race consisting of "Morlocks," who lived underground and tended to the machines that ran the world, and "Eloi," who were refined creatures who breathed fresh air and lived in above-ground structures. Madison Avenue, with its rarefied, pony-tailed creative types dictating commands to gray-faced, underpaid media buying departments, held a strong resemblance to this scenario (and still does).

Additionally, where Madison Avenue is physically located plays a role in its denial. The broadcast networks and agencies that comprise Madison Avenue are located in New York City, which, although a media, financial, and creative powerhouse, has not in recent times been known as a center of technological innovation, even if it is a significant consumer of that technology. Recall that its answer to the revolutionary media changes imposed by the rise of the Internet was Silicon Alley. Regardless of the hype generated by New York's attempt to mirror California's technology economy and Silicon Alley's wealth creativity, with few exceptions its contribution to the evolution of networking technology and new digital marketing paradigms was neither significant nor long-lasting. Most of its dominating companies disappeared as soon as investors decided that Internet-based companies were no longer worthy of financial speculation.

Some of Madison Avenue's problems are certainly generational. Its executive personnel came of age when there was a very simple media model in which the necessary competency consisted of writing compelling copy or concocting arresting thirty-second spots, not in mastering the nuances of interactive marketing. As noted by WPP's Sir Martin Sorrell in WPP's 2005 Annual Report:

> Decision-makers in media owners and agencies tend to be in their fifties and sixties: their sons and daughters and grandchildren are shifting in ever greater numbers to multi-tasking on the web, personal video recorders, video-on-demand, and Internet games. Many leading executives are in denial.

But the peculiarly divided and backward culture of Madison Avenue can't alone explain its failure to shake itself free from denial. In the 1990s, the advertising industry began to consolidate from a handful of independent shops into a handful of gigantic conglomerates. By 2004, six gigantic ad firms—Omnicom, WPP, the Interpublic Group, Grey Global, Havas, and Publicis—controlled 60 percent of advertising spending worldwide. The reason the holding model evolved was simple: it provided a way for the industry to grow without running afoul of one of the advertising industry's most important taboos—that no individual firm could serve competing clients at the same time. But by imposing a holding company model on what in years past was a group of independent shops ruled by firebrands, Madison Avenue inadvertently limited the freedom of these shops to freely experiment—and perhaps fail—when it came time to address the requirements of the new media. The result has been immobility, resistance, and an almost ostrich-like indifference to the recognizably inevitable changes.

Despite its tremendous market power, today Madison Avenue finds itself woefully behind the times. Its approach toward interactive media, particularly search media, is defensive and reactive; the way it buys media is simplistic and archaic; its ability to provide meaningfully success metrics for advertising is nonexistent; and its inability to think beyond the traditional thirty-second-spot model is practically shameful.

How could a proud industry that traditionally has considered itself to be filled with creative and innovative thinkers have so badly failed to adapt its practices in order to evolve with digital media?

1.8 Why Even Great Industries Fail to Adjust to Disruptive Change

Several years ago, Harvard professor Clayton M. Christenson wrote an influential book called *The Innovator's Dilemma* that analyzed how even great companies could fail to master disruptive change. Christenson studied hardware companies in industries subject to rapid changes, both sustaining and disruptive, and came to some important conclusions that directly apply to the current state of the world of advertising. Among them:

1. Small Markets Don't Solve the Growth Needs of Large Companies

Successful companies (such as the ad industry's vast holding companies) have become successful because they have skillfully identified those markets that offer the greatest profit margins, leaving the crumbs to lesser firms. In order to acquire and retain large accounts such as P&G, Coke, Wal-Mart, and the U.S. Army that will generate advertising tonnage, pitched battles are fought between these agencies that will then collect a significant percentage of their revenue by charging fees against a percentage of media spending. By focusing their attention on these large accounts, successful companies concentrate their best resources where it will do most good for their shareholders. Unfortunately, this means that they are naturally not very interested in advertising markets that might be small today, but may be huge in five years.

2. An Organization's Capabilities Define Its Disabilities

Christenson breaks down the capabilities of any organization into processes (the means by which inputs are translated into more valuable outputs) and values (the criteria used by managers to create priorities). It is unquestionable that there are many bright people working in the mainstream world of advertising today who realize that the Internet and other computer-based communications technologies are disruptive and have done their utmost to evangelize (both inside and outside the organization) the need to develop a suitable approach toward it. But Christenson notes that the processes of any organization are much less amenable to change. The inability to change processes, which have evolved over a long period of time, can hamstring an organization even though its people realize that change is necessary. In the advertising industry, examples of inflexible or hard-to-change processes include the media-buying process itself, which rewards the agency for spending all of the client's money regardless of its effectiveness, and the traditional creative processes, which are biased toward the thirty-second spot.

In the advertising industry certain processes, including the "clout" achievable by media buying divisions that are able to use large client budgets to achieve economies of scale in the buying process, have contributed to appearance of large, relatively slow-moving conglomerates dominating this industry. While "bigger is better" provided distinct advantages in the past, the traditional advantages offered by the holding company model may now be offset and negated by the need to move very quickly in response to the ever-multiplying media and media models characteristic of today's media environment.

In all of these cases, the very same processes that made a given company successful can doom it in the face of disruptive change. Unfortunately, it matters very little whether executives aboard companies being attacked by disruptive technologies fully realize that their enterprises are at risk or possess the values required to effect a turnabout. The real problem exists in developing appropriate processes, and it is here that even companies with the best intentions fail. While Madison Avenue's agency professionals are fond of touting the strengths of their unique culture, pointing repeatedly to "thought leaders" and "creative geniuses" with "big ideas" capable of "changing the culture," these qualities are not the same as those required to build a system that actually drives inefficiencies out of tradition-bound, archaic systems. As one commentator neatly put it: "if Madison Avenue can't build it, then Silicon Valley will" (Joe Marchese, MediaPost 11/21/06).

1.9 Solutions for Marketers: Can You Trust Your Ad Agency?

If you're a CMO, this question is one of the most crucial you'll ever face because you know that you're being squeezed between a rock and a hard place. Corporate expectations of your ability to drive enterprise growth have never been higher, and yet, as new forms of marketing media proliferate and morph at increasing speed, your job has grown exponentially more complex. We don't have to tell you what you already know: the average tenure for a CMO is just 23.2 months, about half the tenure of a CEO.

It's possible that television and other untargeted marketing provide enough value to you, regardless that their role in the overall media ecosystem is eroding, rendering these traditional methods as unnecessarily more expensive propositions. Your concerns about scale and reach may have kept you from focusing on just how much money is wasted on untargeted marketing, or that even the most brilliant, creative campaign in the world does nothing if the eyes it seeks are looking elsewhere.

But it's also likely that you may have questions about whether your agency really is ready to enter the next age of media, or whether its methods are wedded to a past that no longer exists.

You are doubtless aware of the extraordinary evolution of the media marketplace, and certainly you realize that a profound shift in strategy and tactics is required in order to master marketing toward a myriad of digitally enabled channels ranging from search advertising to podcasting to video-on-demand to satellite radio. You should expect not just familiarity with these new media issues from your ad agency, but also mastery and fluency. Do not be lulled into thinking that just because your ad agency has a long history of success that it necessarily has the core competencies necessary to maintain that success in the future. While it is true that media evolution was once incremental and that media plans for successive years resembled each other closely, the marketing industry is undergoing a rapid, disruptive, and thorough evolution that requires an equivalent evolution in thought about how media is produced and consumed.

Ask the tough questions, including how "campaign success" will be defined. What kind of technology will they be using to monitor your campaign? Are they relying on simple, sample-based metrics? What metrics beyond reach and frequency will be used to judge it? What kind of quantification will be given to metrics relating to brand involvement and/or engagement? How will interaction effects between divergent forms of media be measured? Unless you are completely convinced that your agency is ready to deal with the multiple new metrics required to evaluate digital media, it's a safe bet that your agency's attitudes, methods, and practices are stuck in the past, which is not a place you can afford to be.

1.10 Solutions for Agencies: Be an Agent of Reform at Your Agency

If you're an advertising professional, you have a vested interest in your agency coming to terms with the world of advertising that is undergoing a radical and unprecedented transformation. And yet you have likely encountered significant obstacles to the urgent need to reform and modify the way your agency thinks about media, the relationship between the creative and the mechanics of delivering it, and the traditional gap between "big idea" people and the number-crunchers.

Reforming the culture of an organization is difficult. Many in your organization likely rose to power when the industry was ruled by an entirely different reality. These folks may be too ingrained in their habits to adjust to entirely new ways of thinking. Unfortunately, the only thing that will change this is a change of guard—when the previous generation retires and relinquishes the reins of power to a younger crowd who understands the critical role that digital marketing plays in effective, integrated marketing campaigns.

If there's hope for this industry, it lies in the wealth of smart people in mainstream advertising who understand that, unless they take some meaningful steps to add value to their agencies, they run the risk of being disintermediated by insurgent forces coming from the outside.

Some steps are already being taken. In October 2006 WPP and CBS took a stake in SpotRunner, an ad automation service that provides low production costs as well as cheap, self-service functionality for advertisers. In December Publicis bought Digitas, a firm known for its digital marketing expertise. Such a combination represents, in the words of one analyst, "the inevitable bridge-building between traditional agency services and the increasing complexities of online marketing." (Leland Westerfield, quoted in the *New York Times*, 12/21/06). In May 2007 WPP went further, buying the digital marketing firm 24/7 Real Media for $649 million.

It isn't too late for Madison Avenue to reform itself, to marry its traditional creative brilliance with the more quantitatively oriented, technologically savvy way of approaching the requirements of media planning and execution for today's world. This synthesis is possible, and its achievement is vital.

CHAPTER 2

Eyestrain

Digital Marketing Isn't Easy (And It Isn't Going to Get Easier)

"Let's look at the facts: They [the search engines] have the best data to understand consumer habits, they can track your search, they know how much time you spend on certain sites. They're doing much more powerful work than some of the work by some of the more traditional agencies."

—Paul Lavoie, Chief Creative Officer of Taxi,
quoted in the *New York Times*, 11/21/06

*

FIRST-GENERATION digital marketing (1994–2000) was simple, employed limited targeting, and used straightforward metrics such as CPM, Reach, and Frequency, all of which were inherited from the analog world. Second-generation digital marketing (2000 onward) is incomparably more complex—and more powerful. Search Engine Marketing adds levels of control and complexity that have never before been seen in the ad marketplace in real time. This is why search marketing is the most daunting yet most advanced method of digital marketing today.

Although digital media deliver unprecedented power and precision to marketers, they also impose a new set of requirements that are difficult to master. The rise of search engines, along with segmentation tools such as demographic and geographical targeting introduced by those engines, has created new forms of nonobtrusive, highly relevant marketing that can be "nanocasted" to small niche audiences. These mass-personalization capabilities will soon be extended to nonsearch media. The complexity of designing, executing, and monitoring such targeted campaigns does come with a price, especially in terms of the human resource costs associated with their administration, but the cost of not moving to targeted relevant media and advertising is one of escalating media waste and reduced advertising effectiveness.

2.1 Digital Marketing Grows Up

In its early years digital marketing was relatively straightforward. Marketers would buy positions on high-traffic sites, paying a few cents, or even a few fractions of a cent, per impression, in the hope that some percentage of users seeing their banner ads would click on them. On the large portal sites that dominated the era, such as ZDNet.com, Time-Warner's Pathfinder, Yahoo, Lycos, and others, there was a crude level of content base. Marketers could buy positions in "channels" (a term borrowed from television, but with a level of targeting more similar to magazines or niche cable channels) that roughly corresponded to a given demographic or interest category that was known to exist from historical data, and allowed for no-brainer media targeting. Existing data about the characteristics of a given magazine audience (say, *People* vs. *Sports Illustrated*, and these vs. *Time*) was used to help gauge the value of running ads on a particular channel. Although some advertisers experimented with cobranded sponsored publishing projects, the bulk of interactive advertising was sold according to this channelized model. Later, ad networks such as DoubleClick.com evolved to serve banner ads in this fashion but across multiple portals and networks of midsize sites.

Notably, these early ad networks did not did not deal with niche-oriented web sites and imposed impression thresholds (typically in the hundreds of thousands per month) that anyone falling below, such as all the small to midsize Web publishers, would not be admitted into their ad-serving networks. The result was a peculiar situation in which only a relatively small set of high-traffic web sites were able to run advertising. Small to midsize sites, which together comprised a large and growing segment of the Web's collective pages, were forced to rely upon affiliate networks, banner link exchanges, and other methods to fund their operations.

In this early era, there was wide disagreement about the effectiveness of banner ads. Users developed "banner blindness" that, over time, resulted in a decline in the average number of site visitors clicking on a given banner ad. Meanwhile, publishers insisted that click-through rates weren't the whole story and that being able to garner a large number of impressions contributed a valuable intangible "branding" aspect, even if that value could not be precisely ascertained. And although many advertisers wondered about whether impressions had much value, online publishers resisted going to a non-CPM model such as CPC (cost-per-click) because it would depress their revenues. Besides, CPM-based digital marketing was so cheap that many marketers didn't mind allocating a tiny fraction of their budgets toward display advertising, just in case the publishers might happen to be right.

Impression-based advertising, sold via CPM, is certainly a less wasteful means of advertising, but the whole idea of CPM—that the best way to sell advertising was to charge per aggregate impressions—began to be challenged when it became apparent that not all impressions are equal. Although many brand-oriented marketers will be willing to tolerate the inherent waste associated with the process of displaying advertising in front of thousands of people, most of whom will not be responsive, some marketers are more interested in doing everything they can to reach specific kinds of people—those most likely to respond to their message and heed their call to action. These advertisers are willing to pay much more in order to reach people who are more likely to purchase their goods and services. Instead of thinking about cost-per-thousand, these advertisers were more interested in setting a value to each individual's action.

Media buyers purchasing CPM inventory became increasingly concerned about the specific pages on which their ads were shown, creating a labor intensive process of validation and reconciliation. Among the issues of critical interest to the media buyers were:

1. Relative click-through rate (comparing placements)
2. Post-click behavior (comparative differences in measured activity after users clicked on ads)
3. Position on the page (above or below the fold)
4. Frequency caps (per user, per creative execution, and cumulative)
5. Page clutter (number of ads)
6. Reconciled ad impressions (publisher vs. third-party ad server)
7. Page content fit to the specified media

True performance-based advertising had yet to arrive, but when it did, it would thoroughly revolutionize the way the effectiveness of advertising was reckoned. It would also create a dazzling new set of methodologies by which digital marketing campaigns could be launched, optimized, and practically perfected in a way that was unprecedented in the marketing world.

2.2 The Rise of Search

When the Internet first made its appearance as a mass phenomenon in the early 1990s, many pundits heralded its arrival by announcing that finally the era of "convergence" had arrived. Digital media would allow for the extension into cyberspace of existing empires in a way that reinforced old media power. Those who controlled both the content and the distribution of their assets would be the new leaders, and vast profits and synergies would be released in this grand convergence

Although there was no such grand convergence, over time the content on the Internet did improve, broaden, and grow into millions of different niches—some of them fanciful, others purely pragmatic. Some of this content came from established media outlets and copyright owners, but a large share of it arose spontaneously from a vast, irregular army of independent publishers (some of whom published as a hobby without goals of earning a substantial revenue from advertising or subscriptions) and from e-commerce merchants who uploaded gigabytes of product information to the Web in order to better describe their offerings to shoppers or to provide online support to existing customers.

The quantity of information being uploaded to the Web and made accessible to the increasing throngs of visitors was growing exponentially, but it was a mass of poorly organized information of varying quality. Enter the search engines, categorizing and sorting through the increasing chaos and clutter. Because their sole purpose was to serve up these nearly infinite divergent channels in meaningful chunks to those who searched through them, the engines made a diverse field of information knowable, explorable, and (eventually) monetizable.

In retrospect, the phenomenal growth of search seems unsurprising because the function of search is so deeply ingrained in the human psyche. Before the first caveman crawled out of his cave, human beings have been searching for things to improve their lives. The urge to find, discover, and explore is programmed into us, and it will continue for as long as we walk the planet. Searching, because it reflects a fundamentally human quest that is unconcerned with whatever form such information takes, be it text, images, graphics, sound files, or other yet-to-be-developed media form, is the most powerful, unifying activity ever formulated by digital media.

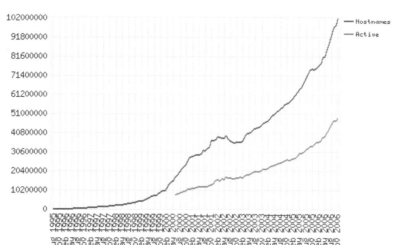

Growth of Internet Sites, 1995–2006. Source: Netcraft.com

Search engines, in primitive form, had been available for many years—in fact, they predated the Web. As early as 1990, Archie, Veronica, and Gopher provided a fairly efficient way for people to get outside and rummage around the increasing torrent of (mostly academic) documents floating in cyberspace. They were then succeeded by the first generation of search engines specifically designed to index web pages: now-forgotten properties such as the World Wide Web Wanderer, Aliweb, WebCrawler, the World Wide Web Worm, and others.

In the Web's early days, web directories were more generally useful than these early search engines, and were the natural successors to link lists, which were simply web pages in which the publisher had embedded resources likely to be of interest to the site's readers. One such list, called "Jerry and David's Guide to the World Wide Web," was launched in early 1994, and later became Yahoo, the dominant directory on the Web today. Other popular general-subject directories included Excite,

Lycos, and Magellen-McKinley, and they were accompanied by many specific-subject directories such as People Finders. Yahoo survived because it was able to expand quickly from its humble directory roots through acquisitions, growing massively and doing everything possible to become what was then called a "sticky hub."

Unlike directories and portals, which were maintained by human editors, search engines were programs run by algorithms, and the first engines were both hard to use and produced highly erratic results. To use them effectively, it was necessary to bone up on Boolean logic and proximity operators (which looked for query terms existing within a user-specifiable character range in any web page), and even then it might produce seemingly endless pages of irrelevant results. One engine would only yield decent results by skillful use of the NEAR (proximity) operator. Another would gag on queries that weren't carefully formatted to adhere to its in-built case sensitivities. Even the best engine, AltaVista, with the largest index, had an annoying habit of spitting out results that were adulterated by long lists of clearly irrelevant queries. The experience was so exasperating that "how to search" books appeared, comparing the engines and recommending how users might best exploit them. For a while, Meta-Search engines (which searched across multiple engines) provided more utility because they raised the odds that one of the engines would produce a relevant result. However, they were cumbersome to use and with many queries all they did was multiply the garbage that the engines were spewing out.

Goto.com, a search engine launched by serial entrepreneur Bill Gross in 1997, heralded the dawn of the CPC (cost-per-click) advertising method. Charging advertisers by the click instead of the impression had been tried before in 1996 (by OpenText, LinkStar, and Yahoo), but Goto.com's implementation of this method was the first widely successful instance of a CPC-based ad model. After users entered a query in the search box, they were exposed to a SERP (Search Engine

Results Page) containing both "natural" search results compiled by the search engine as well as text advertisements generated by the keyword. Goto.com established the basic model by which advertisers were able to gain visibility on SERPs. Keywords were sold in an electronic auction, and the marketer who paid the most would be rewarded with a placement at the top of the page, where the majority of clicks occurred. Marketers were billed not by impression, but by the click.

Many doubted that users would elect to click on these paid placements, but users did because, in many cases, these listings were exactly what they were looking for—especially if the nature of the query was commercial. In 1998, Goto's first year of operation, it booked about $800,000 in revenues. Four years later it would book more than $600 million. Advertisers liked the way it worked, especially its self-serve console, which was simple, straightforward, and capable of providing a near real-time view of the effectiveness of a marketing campaign.

As pointed out by John Battelle in his history of the dawn of search-based advertising, *The Search* (Portfolio, 2006), Goto's way of serving advertising represented a true revolution in the way advertising was thought of, consumed, and produced. Before Goto, advertising, including online advertising, was "attached" to a piece of content. This content might be an article, a web page, or a position on a high-traffic portal, but it was essentially a static element, like a billboard. Furthermore, given that only a small fraction of the viewers would ever act on its call to action, and an even smaller share would ever "convert"—or perform the action requested by the advertiser—this content-attached advertising was wasteful and inefficient . Search-based advertising, however, decoupled advertising's traditional attachment to content and was assembled dynamically and on the fly, answering to the actual intent of the user as evinced by the user's selection of keywords. This created a form of advertising that was:

- less wasteful because the advertiser no longer had to pay for impressions that were not likely to result in consumer action;
- more likely to be acted upon by the user because the ad, coupled to the user's demonstrated intent, was more relevant to what he or she had in mind; and
- more profitable to publishers, given that they could now offer traffic that, differentiated by a search engine, could be matched to multiple advertisers willing to pay much more for it than for undifferentiated traffic.

As Battelle points out, Goto, not Google, was the real inventor of this revolutionary way of serving advertising, and the story behind how Goto (which became Overture, which was later acquired by Yahoo) failed to capitalize on this innovation is a complicated and somewhat tragic story. Suffice it to say that Goto.com was always dependant on external partners (Microsoft and Yahoo) to serve the traffic it needed in order to monetize its site, whereas Google already had the traffic and, once it had cloned Goto's technology to serve up paid results along with its organic results, was able to turn itself into a cash machine.

Google, launched in 1999, was first and foremost a search engine, and its major innovation lay in the addition of a proprietary popularity-ranking factor to the traditional full-text search engine technology then in use. This factor, called PageRank, took account of the number and quality of incoming links to any given web page or site in order to help ascertain its objective merit. PageRank, when factored in with other elements of a given web page that indicate relevance, produced search results that were astonishingly pertinent, almost as if they had been evaluated by a very wise and careful human being before being presented to the user. Google's relevancy engine (which now includes many additional relevancy-weighing factors) was so much better than those offered by competing engines that it quickly became the preferred search engine among many Web users. It also attracted the attention of several large portals, including AOL/Netscape, a development that caused Google's query traffic to grow beyond 3 million searches per day by 1999 (official Google History Page, http://www.google.com/corporate/history.html).

As a result of its laserlike focus, Google's popularity with users continued to grow exponentially. As news traveled virally through cyberspace about how well the stripped-down, sparse-looking engine worked, by mid-2000 Google's query volume rose to 18 million daily queries.

Google's founders were aware of Goto.com, but until 2001 believed that the addition of paid search results would alienate Google's growing flock of users. Rejecting a partnership offer from Gross, they launched AdWords, a Web-based, self-service ad platform that worked very similarly to Goto by allowing marketers to quickly compose text ads, bid on keywords, and enter the advertising business for just $5.00. Over the next two years Google expanded its distribution greatly, including to portal powerhouse AOL whose 34 million members vastly increased the reach of marketers using AdWords. In 2003, in order to maximize the distribution possibilities for AdWords-placed CPC ads, Google launched a contextual advertising product and soon thereafter acquired Applied Semantics, a four-year-old company based in Santa Monica, California. The Google technology was integrated into Applied Semantic's Adsense, a program allowing Web publishers, both large and small, to begin monetizing their site traffic through the display of contextually targeted ads. Applied Semantics technology, combined with Google's keyword-driven advertising marketplace, became a huge incremental revenue source for Google, thereby extending its money-making reach beyond search. This allowed Google, through partnerships with web site owners large and small, to begin monetizing the remaining time a user spent online.

In effect, advertising-supported search engines eliminated two traditional barriers to electronic media advertising that had existed since electronic media's inception. The first barrier was the threshold amount of money that marketers needed to have on hand in order to be advertisers. Even tiny marketers who had never seriously thought of doing digital marketing could afford the modest $5.00 entry fee. The second barrier, the traffic thresholds required by the big online ad networks in order to run advertising on web pages, had kept small Web publishers from running advertising because their web pages lacked sufficient traffic.

And there was a third barrier eliminated, although it would be several years before it became evident. Google and Goto, almost without knowing what they had done, had changed advertising from what had traditionally been the domain of the agencies, specialists, media buyers, and broadcasters, and put its power firmly in the hands of the people. Google had made advertising something available to everyone, much like what Charles Schwab had done with the buying and selling of stocks. Geeky marketers were the first to tap the power of the Goto and Google marketplaces. Interactive media agencies and search marketing firms such as my firm, Didit.com, recognizing that the search engines would continue to monetize their traffic, expanded their focus from search engine optimization to the management and optimal deployment of paid search campaigns. Plus, the CPCs in the early years of PPC search marketing were so low that anyone with a reasonable level of smarts could run a profitable campaign.

In the next few years, the technology used by Google to run its ad auctions continued to evolve rapidly. After it became a public company, Google faced new pressures from Wall Street to post continually growing earnings, and it took aggressive steps to both expand its ability to seek new sources of revenue and to more efficiently monetize that revenue from the PPC ad marketplace that had originally made it a dominant powerhouse. It began adding additional factors to the ad-ranking system in order to better predict an ad's relevance (as measured by predicted Click-Through Rate, or CTR), moving beyond simple historical keyword performance to include an examination of the relevance of the ad's copy to its associated keyword, match type, domain name, landing page, and other variables that enhanced the relevancy of search results for its users. These changes all were intended to provide more user-relevant search results, thus producing higher overall click-through rates on ads and simultaneously improving Google's revenues as well as the searcher's user experience..

Google's ability to monetize its PPC marketplace represents an amazing achievement. While it did not invent the auction-based PPC marketplace, its continual refinements to both its organic algorithms and its ad-serving technology distinguished it against its competitors, notably Yahoo, which bought the originator of paid-placement search ads Goto.com after Goto had had gone public as Overture. Yahoo was quite familiar with Overture—having used Goto as the back-end technology and platform powering the paid-placement portion of the Yahoo results)—as well as Microsoft, which did not deploy an auction-based ad server until 2005. Google, however, improved the Goto/Overture platform by factoring in the predicted click-through rate of an ad when determining position—not simply running a pure auction. Google could not have achieved the level of steady, aggressive growth demanded by Wall Street without moving away from the pure-auction model and squeezing every possible efficiency from its PPC marketplace.

To those who bought its stock early (it was initially offered at $85), a considerable bounty was realized (at the time of this writing, Google's share price had topped $500.00), and yet Google's dominance of the emergent digital marketplace was not without controversy. Copyright holders accused it of essentially using their content (or at least snippets of it) to sell advertising, thus effecting a transfer of wealth that, if not exactly illegal, was immoral. Madison Avenue watched Google's growing power with alarm, especially after Google made several conspicuous announcements signaling its intention to be the central access point for all the world's information. Even the marketers who had flocked to AdWords because it provided an efficient method of acquiring customers or selling products began to have reservations about the way Google conducted its marketplace, noting that Google's business model depended upon selling clicks, not sales, leads, subscriptions, or goods.

Even while the number of search queries grew modestly, Google's revenue grew at significant multiples due to their focus on relevance-driven advertising and global marketplace expansion, which was geared toward not just search, but also its contextual advertising network. Many of the millions of dollars flowing into the Google, Yahoo, and Microsoft coffers were being reallocated from other media typically controlled by Madison Avenue agencies. As many ad agencies drag

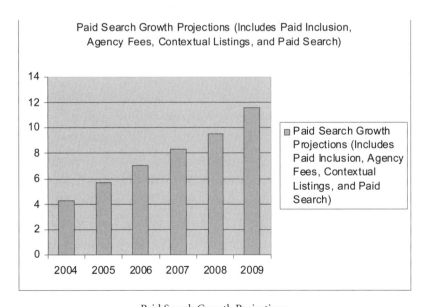

Paid Search Growth Projections

their feet, uncomfortable with buying media in real-time auctions that are based not on demographics but rather keywords, and without the benefit of graphical ads, the search money machine rolls steadily forward, with or without Madison Avenue.

2.3 Search Engines Morph into Media Exchanges

Google's expansion in 2003 into contextual advertising was its first foray into nonsearch advertising, even if it was keyword based (contextual targeting). In 2005 and 2006, Google made numerous moves indicating its intention to aggressively bring the benefits of its ad platform to nonsearch and even nononline media. These moves greatly worried the media establishment, whose executives correctly perceived that search engines, after inventing a new form of digital marketing effective enough to begin siphoning advertising dollars from its coffers, were now quite possibly directing their attention toward actually disintermediating the entire advertising industry. Google believes—and is willing to put its money in play to prove—that online media marketplaces provide advertisers with access to media more efficiently than the current status quo. That may not be true for all media assets, but clearly paid-placement search proved that valuable advertising assets could be monetized through a real-time auction marketplace.

In January 2006, Google acquired radio station automation vendor dMarc. dMarc owned several proprietary technologies that are currently being used by radio stations in the United States. These technologies include DataServices, a system managing the flow of textual information transmitted alongside traditional AM and FM radio signals to RDS (Radio Data Systems) and HD radio–capable receivers, and RevenueSuite, a system for automatically inserting paid commercials into open and unsold radio airtime, allowing broadcasters to effortlessly monetize airtime that would otherwise go unsold.

This was a clear shot across the bow of the media-buying arms of advertising agencies. In effect, Google was announcing itself to be a new media network open to both agencies and marketers directly where media wasn't negotiated but rather auctioned. Some agencies felt that Google clearly intended to cut them out of the business: in an e-mail to Google AdWords advertisers, Google disclosed:

> the new service will *connect advertisers directly to radio stations* through its automated processes. This technology seeks to simplify the sales process, scheduling, delivery and reporting of radio advertising, in an effort to help advertisers more efficiently purchase and track their campaigns. In addition, the service *connects advertisers directly to creative and production talents* for this creation of radio ads. By helping to increase the ease of implementation and accountability of radio spots, this platform seeks to bring greater ROI to advertisers nationwide. (italics added)

While dMarc's system was designed for radio, its back-end is also suitable for the trafficking and auto-insertion of podcasts, online video, and, most important, cable television ads. And if anyone still wondered about what Google's intentions were, they only had to listen to Eric Schmidt, its CEO, when he spoke at a conference of publishing executives in the spring of 2006:

> No one is suggesting that we're going to take that old analog 13-channel black and white RCA television you have in the basement and make that into a vibrant advertising device, but virtually everyone here in the room has some form of set-top box that's connected to your cable or to your satellite television in your home or apartment here in the city. It's easy enough to know who's family, what street address, what neighborhood, the demographics of you and so on.

Those ads will convert an awful lot better than traditional broad advertising. That's what we're doing. And those businesses are billion-dollar businesses.

In that same summer of 2006, Google raised eyebrows again when it presented a research paper entitled "Social- and Interactive-Television Applications Based on Real-Time Ambient-Audio Identification." In it Google outlined a plan for a system that would connect television, radio, and other conventional media platforms with the Web. It described a complete system that had already been tested and judged to operate successfully, although it was clearly in pre-Beta stage. Still, it showed how deeply Google had thought about how its various technologies could be applied toward the problem of indexing, integrating, and monetizing "old media" content.

Any doubts that Google had Madison Avenue in its crosshairs vanished when, in August, it announced it would begin serving ads to the 7 million subscriber XM satellite radio network. As the press release noted: "Google's technology *automatically schedules and inserts advertising* across XM's non-music commercial channels, helping to increase revenue with a wealth of new advertisers, while *decreasing the costs previously associated with processing advertisements.*" (italics added)

Every move that it has made since has been directed toward extending its reach to touch all possible media. Although the inroads into offline media have not been significant, Google's vision is clear and breathtaking: one day soon, anyone, anywhere in the world will be able to use Google's self-serve advertising technology to place ads in any digitally distributed media, traditional or nontraditional.

It is this possibility—that in one fell swoop Google will take the whole advertising industry and sweep it into the dustbin of history—that is giving the old-school ad men nightmares. Today, uttering the word "Google" in the presence of ad men has the same effect that mentioning the word "cancer" has in a doctor's waiting room. "I have never seen such fear and loathing strike the ad business" confessed one ad exec to *Advertising Age*. Such fear and loathing is not misplaced, nor is the threat that Google poses accidental. The truth is advertising has always been inefficient: what's new is that finally technology is beginning to be able to not only determine *how* inefficient it's been, but also to provide a way to make it decidedly more efficient.

2.4 Increased Power, Increased Complexity

Search, or query-based advertising, is the ultimate "pull marketing" medium. Prospects, many of them in-market, come to marketers in search of products or solutions with the intent to learn more about them and, in a significant share of cases, to consummate a transaction. The way search works has been likened to a "psychic mailman" who magically knocks on your door with an offer from CompUSA at the exact moment you are thinking about buying a new laser printer.

Unlike intrusive media that generates interest and creates curiosity that then leads to demand, search marketing provides advertisers with the opportunity to engage the customer in discourse at the instant when demand manifests itself in the form of a search query.

Search marketing is designed to grab the attention of forward-leaning, involved, information-seeking people who are attempting to find satisfaction—either immediate or delayed—from millions of possible sources. It is unique because it provides for a mode of producing marketing messages that is practically the antithesis of traditional advertising's intrusiveness and irrelevance. Users click on paid ads voluntarily and select from among competing offerings, and the winner is deemed to be the marketer most likely to satisfy a user's conscious need. And perhaps the most revolutionary aspect is that message exchanges are initiated by the customer, not the marketer.

All three stakeholders in the advertising chain are served very well with this form of advertising. Advertisers tap a nonintrusive advertising channel with far less waste; publishers are rewarded by delivering qualified individuals to advertisers, for which they are paid more highly; and consumers are liberated from intrusive, irrelevant ads.

Chris Anderson's influential book, *The Long Tail* (Hyperion, 2006), provided insight into the way that mass niche markets such as the type we find today on the World Wide Web are achieving parity with undifferentiated ones. Historically, serving the demand for specialized products or services has proven too costly to deliver in physical environments. For example, even the biggest big-box retail store only has shelf space for perhaps 100,000 products. In a virtual world, however, with "infinite shelf space," the collective demand for such niche products becomes a significant economic factor. Search engines, by collecting, grading, and cataloging information on all the products, services, and content that the search engine spiders can find, provide a way for users to learn about and acquire such niche products. Thus, they are forces enabling such a "long tail economy" to flourish and grow.

The phenomenon of the long tail characterizes the distribution of search terms. Of the millions of searches performed each day, a small number of them appear in the "head," with the vast majority being distributed along the tail. These keyword searches are not performed very often, but, given that they often consist of keyword combinations exhibiting specific intent to buy or otherwise take advantage of a marketer's services, they may provide a much higher conversion rate. All the search engines provide mechanisms by which marketers can target these low-volume, high-value searches. Because of the specificity of tail-search terms that tend to correlate well to the final stages of buyer behavior—which are the last stages of the buying funnel—many search marketers make the mistake of focusing almost exclusively on those late-stage keywords. But the optimal campaigns, the ones that go beyond the obvious, are true search engine marketing campaigns, not ones that simply assign all the value of the advertising to the last search and click. Later in this book we will further discuss the concept of media modeling.

Additionally, Google, Yahoo, and Microsoft all provide features that allow marketers to precisely target users based upon other criteria that increase power and complexity. Microsoft and Yahoo have both rolled out limited demographic targeting based upon user-supplied data drawn from their subscription networks and often combined with information that can be extracted in real time from an individual's IP address. Microsoft includes age and gender as well as geography, while Yahoo currently supports only geography within its search targeting system. Although Google allows for demographic selections to be made for advertisements placed on the "site targeting" segment of its contextual network, Google's demographic matches are made using general site data provided by comScore, a third-party measurement firm, while geographic profiling is done exclusively based upon IP address. All three engines offer marketers the ability to geo-target— although at various levels of precision—with the lowest common denominator being DMA (Designated Market Area), which is generally precise enough for any major marketer. In addition to targeting by demographics, all three engines allow marketers to daypart or use day-of-week segmentation—although, as of this writing, in Yahoo's case this feature is only available from third-party campaign management vendors who access Yahoo's system through an API (Application Programming Interface). All this incremental targeting may seem like overkill, but it can be critical in segmenting out the most profitable and relevant portions of the search audience. Using segmentation and targeting, marketers can reach those users most likely to act on their offers. These targeting technologies, when combined with prudent keyword selection, provide marketers with the ability to slice, dice, and segment audiences with granular precision. Sound complicated? When a single keyword in Microsoft's adCenter can have more than 7,000 different keyword bid permutations—it is.

For marketers, the rise of search engine marketing created a marketplace of unparalleled power and potential as well as a degree of control never before seen in marketing. Yet this marketplace is also one that, because of the way it operates, is filled with unexpected and mind-numbing complexities. While simple search campaigns may be based upon a handful of keywords, complex campaigns typically involve keywords numbering in the hundreds to upward of a million. Each of these keywords can be programmed to respond to multiple inputs from the engine serving it, such as dayparting, geographic, demographic, and other inputs. The result is a complex, dynamic ad-buying and ad-serving environment with multiple variables, each of which needs to be managed in order to yield the best results to the marketer. This is an exceedingly high maintenance task and requires technology for all but the most simple campaigns. Failure to use the right technology and strategies has caused several highly visible companies to report publicly that they can't make search engine marketing profitable.

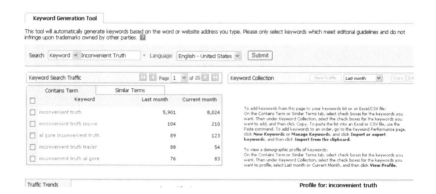

Demographic Targeting Capabilities (Microsoft AdCenter): Microsoft's AdCenter Provides Marketers with Demographic Targeting Capabilities.

Demographic Targeting (Google)

Auction-driven ad marketplaces impose unusual rules that depart markedly from the traditional operations of negotiation-based media marketplaces. The inventory available for sale in the pure paid-placement search marketplace is limited: after all, there are only so many search queries for any given word or phrase each day, month, and year. This fact drives marketers to engage in a constant real-time bidding war, relentlessly attempting to obtain the top positions on the SERPs most able to drive the high-quality search traffic. It also creates what is essentially a "zero-sum" game among the market participants: in order

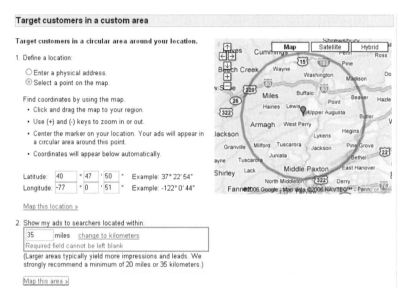

Geotargeting (Google)

for marketer A to obtain these top traffic-driving positions and "win the game," marketer B must lose access to that traffic.

There are two kinds of marketers at the top of the paid placement keyword auctions: brilliant marketers and irrational lunatics. It is impossible for either to know if their competitors are bidding rationally, based on profit or ROI-based formulae, or just throwing money at a PPC search because they have deep pockets.

Because search marketing is filled with so many choices, it is imperative that each marketer make the right one in regard to keywords, engines, titles, descriptions, landing pages, bid prices, and segmentation strategies. Otherwise, he or she will lose ground to a competitor who has the means to optimize all of these choices. Executing all of these campaign-setup and management tasks expertly is, for many marketers, not only a mission-critical requirement with a direct and measurable effect on one's bottom line, but also a major organizational

Dayparting (Microsoft Adcenter)

challenge. The latter is especially true given not only the way marketing departments have been historically silo'd from other business divisions, but also because of the difficulty of finding, training, and overseeing enough qualified people to carry out expert search campaigns. Paid placement search engine marketing reached critical mass in 2003—a year or so before the Google IPO—and has since rocketed in popularity, although growth has dramatically outpaced the availability of skilled search advertising tacticians. Perhaps even more worrisome is that a strong search tactician is necessary to intelligently interview a candidate who will be working in paid-placement search.

Innovation at the search engines is far from over. The engines are tasked with both squeezing additional juice from their lemon (making more revenue from a fixed set of daily searches) and adding additional inventory to their marketplaces through new publisher/broadcaster relationships. The first is achieved through a combination of both a brutal auction marketplace as well as additional targeting. The second—

network expansion—is achieved by leveraging the large pool of ready advertisers and the centralized targeting and billing infrastructure in order to convince new publishers to participate.

The ability to carry out the kind of intensive and ongoing educational program necessary in order to keep pace with the changes that the engines have planned can be challenging for even the most forward-thinking organization. This is one reason why the outsourcing of these tasks has been popular among many businesses seeking to deploy search-based marketing campaigns. But what makes this task especially daunting is that search marketing is a mercurial and unpredictable medium that requires constant adjustment of strategy and tactics. Not only are the search engines' algorithms constantly being refined and the competitive environment perpetually shifting, but the introduction of new targeting technologies also creates thousands of possible permutations, even from just one keyword. These realities require practitioners to be constantly upgrading their skill sets.

Even more daunting is that search marketing is beginning to break out of its traditional browser-PC paradigm. Today, the vast bulk of queries being made through search engines are by those using browsers, mice, and personal computers. This situation is likely to continue for some time, and marketers would be foolish to ignore the imperative to be where the traffic is. But the SERP paradigm of multiple results displayed on a web page will certainly change as search functionality moves into new devices. The most obvious example of this is seen in mobile cell phone browsers, in which the 1024 x 768 browser window is reduced to a tiny fraction of a monitor's screen size. In order to be readable on these tiny screens, text size must be proportionally expanded, thereby reducing the number of results, either organic or sponsored, that can be displayed per any given query. Because the cost of not being number one is far steeper on a cell phone than it is on a computer monitor, this compression will reinforce the pressure on marketers to achieve top-ranked positions. This remains true regardless of whether the call-to-action is a click (PPC advertising) or a paid call.

Although the sophisticated segmentation provided by search engines provides advertisers with powerful targeting possibilities, the complexity of designing, executing, and monitoring such targeted campaigns comes with a price, especially in the costs associated with engineering them. The old ad agency billing model, which typically applies a fixed percentage against total media costs, may not accurately reflect the amount of labor, time, and expense associated with this kind of campaign development, particularly if the agency is going to constantly test changes in campaign structure or user experience in an effort to gain profitably additional scale from a fixed pool of search queries. In this environment, ROI (return on investment) or ROAS (Return on Ad Spend) provides more meaningful indexes than CPM and should be used to evaluate the effectiveness of one's ad dollars. However, as we'll discuss in the next chapter, these direct-response advertising success metrics don't tell the whole story. Worse yet, excessive reliance on direct response ROI metrics can result in a failure to maximize enterprise profit by ignoring how consumers make initial- and repeat-buying decisions.

Solutions

In our view, building an organization's search competency is a key ingredient in successful twenty-first-century marketing. As search (and all the media managed through search engines' targeting technology) becomes more widely accepted as a strategic business objective, more senior managers will recognize that they are doing their stakeholders a disservice by underinvesting in it. They will then do one of two things: either invest properly in their in-house teams in order to apply the kind of steady, specialized focus required to deploy, test, and fine-tune smart

PPC campaigns, or outsource this process to an agency with the analytical skills and technologies necessary. While in-house teams will continue to handle many SEM (Search-Engine Marketing) responsibilities in the near future, many industry analysts believe that outsourcing will increase due to both the escalating complexities of the marketplace as well as the highly competitive PPC bidding environments in the engines, particularly as CPM media join CPC. As the digital media landscape evolves, in-house marketing teams will continue to play a vital role in the effective creation and management of ad campaigns, but their tasks will become increasingly focused on the intersection of analytics, business intelligence, and marketing.

2.5 Solutions: Get Help from a Best-of-Breed Agency

Advertising agencies, whether traditional or interactive, can often make serious errors when attempting to engineer and deploy search campaigns. Yet some agencies do things right. Let's focus on the best practices, and contrast these with potentially incorrect practices.

Understand the Big Picture

Smart agencies understand that they must think about search-engine marketing holistically. *All* advertising and PR activities must be tracked and factored into SEM campaign strategies. Research shows that both online and offline advertising drives search activity.

When advertising is heavy, customers become curious, and they turn to search engines for more information. Similarly, when PR or news coverage spikes, search inventory often surges as well. By understanding the media and PR interaction effects on search, an agency can act as a central hub, coordinating and adjusting SEM campaigns accordingly. In Chapter 4, we will discuss how search-engine marketing data may actually be a powerful metric to gauge the effectiveness of the core portion of the marketing plan, including advertising and PR.

Sell Results, Not Position

Agencies must resist the temptation to be purely position-focused when pitching clients on paid search. A results-focused campaign boosts the client's bottom line. By deemphasizing position, an agency allocates the budget where it works hardest, regardless of whether the campaign objectives are branding or direct response-style metrics. Platforms such as Google AdWords are not designed for position-centered campaigns, and only pressure from less savvy agencies has made Google add a feature that allows marketers to enable position preference. If the combination of your bid and predicted click-through rate (in Google's case they call it a "quality score") is insufficient to get you a position, your ad will not run at all. This is in contrast to the regular Google AdWords system that simply ranks ads in order of relevance-driven yield (bid multiplied by the predicted click-through rate). Using skilled guidance and technology, the invisible AdWords bidding landscape can be finely tuned to balance visibility, click volume, ROI, and even net-predicted enterprise profit.

For Big Campaigns, Broaden Engine and Keyword Selection

Agencies with clients' best interests at heart must resist the temptation to use only a handful of high-volume, easy-to-manage keywords. Large keyword lists and multiple engines (rather than high-volume keywords in one or two engines) allow a smart agency to mine keyword-listing gold. A single campaign can choose forty to one hundred keywords, and the best agencies expand keyword lists to include longer phrases, which not only to gain volume, but also to increase relevance and effectiveness. Typically, with the exception of brand names and model number/names, the longer the search query, the surer the marketer and search engine can be about that searcher's intent and mission. Better agencies that are given a fixed budget or a specific ROI goal know how to tap into these searchers who are closer to a buying decision, deliver high ROI and value, and run broad, balanced campaigns that exploit "the long tail" of search. In Chapter 5 we'll discuss how measured ROI alone may be a shortsighted and insufficiently complex marketing objective, although many marketers will feel the pressure to start their search campaigns using exclusively direct-response metrics.

Demonstrate Match-Type Proficiency

Digital media managers running search, contextual, or behavioral campaigns based upon keywords must leverage the different match types available at each paid-placement engine. Yahoo has two match types: standard and advanced, the latter being a combination of phrase and broad match. Yahoo does not directly offer the ability to set bids differently by match type, but marketers (or their agencies) seeking that level of control can create campaign structures accordingly. Google and Microsoft's match types are controlled within the AdGroup, where each keyword can have a match type specified, along with a bid. Google, Yahoo, and Microsoft all allow negative keywords to be attached to each ad unit, ensuring that a broad match listing attracts targeted traffic and provides searchers with a good user experience, which tends to then deliver high ROI for marketers. Once again, the common thread at the search engines is that, by exerting incremental targeting control, all the players in the ecosystem benefit.

It takes time and strategic thought to use all match types correctly, but the investment pays for itself. Make sure your agency knows how to tap match-type power.

Understanding Marketplaces

Each engine has relationships between CPC/position/conversion/volume as well as ROI tradeoffs that come with changes in the spending/budget. In almost all other online media, as the budget with a specific media property (insertion order) rises, the CPM or CPC decreases in the negotiations. But in paid-placement SEM, contextual, or behavioral media marketplaces, the reverse is true. Media buyers must understand the relationships between price, position, and volume (scale of clicks) that are obtained in all paid-placement venues. All the search engines are running auctions where a particular listing's position is not guaranteed nor predictable to a high level of certainty. Navigating these marketplaces requires an understanding of concepts such as elasticity, game theory, the winner's curse, auctions, equilibria, and, given the irrational behavior of some bidders, perhaps psychology.

Use the Right Technology for the Right Job

Search engine marketing is different from other forms of online marketing. This is because more variables contribute to its success or failure, and the control of these variables occurs nearly in real time. Agencies that truly want to ensure client success understand that the right technology can make a huge difference in both the time required to manage a campaign as well as the campaign's success. Some agencies—and even a few large marketers—are tied directly to the search-engine servers (computers) through an Application Programming Interface (API) that allows for large campaigns to be manipulated far more easily than would be possible through the standard Web-based login. Larger, more complex campaigns especially benefit dramatically from these API-driven campaigns. For any technology to do its job it needs to know what to optimize for (have measurable campaign objectives). In Chapter 6 we discuss the specifics of technology and its corresponding impact on digital media.

Go the Extra Mile

Marketers rely on their agencies to provide new opportunities while also executing the best possible campaigns using preselected media. Successful agencies go beyond creative development and media-spend allocation. They learn about the best SEM practices, create best practices of their own, research new media opportunities, understand the contextual inventory issues, explore common issues that impact a large set of marketers (their clients), and aggregate the knowledge and expertise of a large team. All this is in addition to developing an understanding of the client's business, challenges, objectives, and metrics.

If agencies want to play in search and the other highly targetable media making its way into the search-engine marketplaces (auctions), they must get serious. If they don't, marketers will create in-house SEM divisions or they will continue looking for the agency that has the expertise and technology required to maximize profit in an increasingly complex ecosystem. Any agency that doesn't take SEM and auctioned media seriously should not be given the responsibility of planning and executing these campaigns, because, otherwise, the results can be disastrous.

2.6 Solutions: Build Your Organization's Search Competency

Search marketing is becoming a crucial cornerstone of any modern, multichannel marketing campaign. Someday—and it might be sooner than many expect—search marketing will be taught as part of a business, marketing, or advertising curriculum at business schools, undergraduate institutions, and perhaps even in secondary schools. For the moment, however, finding qualified people who can plan and execute search campaigns is a great challenge. Most of the time they are simply pulled from other departments. In fact, a 2006 Jupiter Survey reported that many people doing in-house SEM work share these duties with up to five other job functions, including web site design (58 percent), e-mail advertising (57 percent), marketing communications (49 percent), market research (44 percent), and banner advertising (38 percent). A few unlucky souls even shared PPC campaign management duties with print, radio, and outdoor advertising responsibilities. Due to a shortage of educational resources, or educational resources that leave out critical knowledge and skim the surface in the hopes of closing the gap, most have learned their skills on the job. Unfortunately, many of those learning this way are not learning best practices, but are instead picking up a tip, trick, or tactic from a book, blog, or conference without a comprehensive understanding of how particular tactics apply to their business specifically. As with other types of media and advertising, not all tactics or strategies are appropriate for every campaign.

These findings are a recipe for two really bad things. The first is employee burnout. The more hats these search-marketing professionals have to wear, particularly given the ever-increasing media, the more they are likely to be experiencing burnout. The second is underperforming search campaigns that are the result of their responsibility being assigned to overburdened, unfocused, and insufficiently trained people. Unfortunately, the findings suggest that there is a deep disconnect between the top-level executives in corporate America (who know or *should* know that having competency in search marketing is becoming essential to achieving strategic business goals) and the people further down on the organization chart who are managing the day-to-day operations of these enterprises, hiring people, and controlling HR budgets. These top-level executives appear to regard search as a sim-ple—perhaps even trivial—task to be added to an employee's daily schedule. It's not unusual to see clerical staff with little or no training managing paid search and auction media campaigns. Equally perplex-ing, however, is finding the CEO or company owner spending nights, weekends, and critically important business hours managing the com-pany's paid search.

This is not to say that there aren't a few exceptional people out there who can do all of their disparate duties equally well, or that a full-time staff is needed in order to manage SEM competently. Small campaigns with limited objectives can certainly be accomplished with one or more talented full- or part-time employees. Larger campaigns, however, that are running hundreds of thousands of keywords through multiple search engines will naturally require a higher level of internal commitment, including an investment in technology to help with the number crunching. Without knowing more about the size of the companies represented in the Jupiter survey, it's impossible to generalize precisely about how badly these internal SEM teams are underfunded or underresourced. But the findings do suggest that cor-porate America is being penny-wise and pound-foolish when it comes to search.

Believing that in-house teams can run successful search campaigns manually is a common mistake made by many organizations. While this is technically possible for small campaigns with a limited number of keywords, it's a recipe for failure for any search campaign that takes advantage of the sophisticated targeting technologies used by the engines today. There are, however, many off-the-shelf campaign man-agement tools that can help replace the time-consuming manual cam-paign management tasks that can make running PPC campaigns an insufferable grind, providing at least some relief for those struggling to run campaigns manually. But be aware that it is impossible for any technology vendor to provide an "off-the-shelf" tool that's going to automatically make a campaign profitable, and most of these tools or technologies are not customizable to the needs of individual businesses. Also, no matter how good the tool, any campaign can always be more efficient and profitable. Tools, however valuable, will never be aware of the details of an individual business's operations, its competitive landscape, or its business goals, but instead must be operated skillfully by those who are. Any technology is only as good as the technicians and strategists using it.

To manage search, highly trained people who can "drive" this technology competently are needed, as well as very smart people who can interpret the data the campaign creates and then use that data to continually refine the way the campaign is run. This is a tall order, even with the best technology and the best people. After all, with the advanced segmentation tools being rolled out by all the engines, each keyword can have thousands of permutations. In a real-time auction marketplace in which competitors freely enter and exit the market, the tactical environment literally changes from minute to minute, which means that campaigns may also need to be monitored and adjusted in real time. Training is key for in-house SEM teams, just as it is for the professionals at digital agencies. The search engines, including Google, actively provide up-to-date information on the important issues affecting the search marketplace. Organizations such as SEMPO (the Search Engine Marketing Professional Organization), the DMA (Direct Marketing Association), and other for-profit enterprises are working to create more and better training materials for new entrants to the market. Because this industry is so short-staffed—which is mainly because the skill sets required for practitioners are so specialized—training is key. Someday, we may see courses in search marketing added to undergraduate and graduate business courses, but, for now, none of us can afford to wait until then.

Marketers who choose to staff internal SEM and digital marketing departments face another real risk: employee turnover. The shortage of skilled, knowledgeable staff has caused a combination of salary escalation and high turnover. When all the knowledge regarding search campaigns resides with a chosen few, the loss of one or more of these employees can have devastating consequences.

2.7 Solutions: Successful Digital Marketing Means Investing in Data

The words "Who, What, When, Where, and Why" are drummed into journalism students when they learn about how to construct news stories. From a digital marketing perspective, given that technology now allows one to gain insight into these questions, these "Five W's" are also especially important. While technology does not allow marketers to know exactly who is clicking on their ads, or why exactly they clicked on it, the what, when, and where can be known, allowing the ability to make powerful inferences about the who and the why.

One important fact that many new entrants to the search marketplace do not seem to realize is the degree to which the success of their campaigns depends upon accumulating enough historical data to make these and other inferences. Some come armed with a great deal of information about their customer's historical behavior (including when they are in-market, where they are located, and what types of messages they are most likely to respond to), and from the outset, this information naturally helps them achieve better-than-average campaign results.

But others must buy their way in to this knowledge, and the only way to do so is to buy a bunch of keywords, throw up a campaign, and, assuming the right measurement and metrics technology is in place, let the numbers roll in. After enough clicks have occurred over a long enough period of time to comprise a statistically valid sample, the marketer can begin to make some informed decisions about what needs to be done to maximize conversions. Naturally, the more money allocated to the exploratory stage, the quicker these conclusions can be made and the conversion optimization process can begin.

For these marketers who must buy their way in to the optimization process, it might seem unfair that the search engines—each of which has a treasure trove of historical data pertaining to the way that keywords, campaign structures, and dayparting strategies influence conversion behavior—do not share this intelligence with marketers buying keywords from them. One reason often given for this is that every business is different and what worked for others may not be appropriate in every instance. Unfortunately, the degree to which the engines disclose data regarding what works within specific industry segments isn't likely to increase anytime soon. In fact, as the auction marketplaces become more opaque, all of the engines seem to be moving in the opposite direction. Only through sophisticated trial-and-error techniques can a system even predict the change in CPC required to effect a change in position, which may even be fleeting as competitors react to the changes they observe and counteract.

That historical data has real, strategic value should not be lost on those using agencies to manage their search campaigns. Who owns this data? The agency (which typically administers the account) or the marketer? What will happen to this data if the marketer decides to switch agencies, which occurs frequently in the SEM business? These are thorny issues that should be discussed before any deal is closed. Regardless of who owns the data, the insights and knowledge gained from that data always stays with the agency. Agencies that accumulate and analyze data from dozens of advertisers are more adept at how to put that data to use. They achieve critical mass and become more valuable because of their knowledge, And all their clients benefit from the combined data scale.

Historical information can give marketers excellent insight into the Five W's, but its real power comes when this data is used with a campaign automation system that first makes use of this data to predictively model future keyword, daypart, geographic, and click parameters; second, matches that data against offer performance; and then aggressively bids for those audience segments that are most likely to convert. In this scenario, historical data doesn't just provide a path toward determining the Five W's, but it is actually the raw material from which future search profits are forged.

CHAPTER 3

Eyes Wide Shut
The Media Plan Is Obsolete

"The reality is that there is absolutely an almost infinite number of choices that media agencies have to choose from. And I think that sadly, the machinery that agencies and the marketers that hire them have at their disposal are rusty and are archaic"

—Tim Hanlon, Senior Vice President, Ventures, Denuo, speaking at the Digital Hollywood Conference, 10/24/06

*

IN THE PAST, media planning decisions were characterized by long lead times and a limited set of programming or media choices. Advertisers were willing to hand over billions of dollars to broadcasters, publishers, and networks without any guarantees. But now, this slow-moving world has been overtaken by one in which audiences move quickly and marketers no longer have the luxury of revisiting their media allocation decisions once or twice a year. This new world requires both a new information infrastructure that eliminates friction in the media buying process as well as a more fluid way for marketers to allocate advertising spending in order to exploit fast-rising media opportunities while simultaneously improving message targeting and relevance.

3.1 Digital Media Is Hard to Plan For

In the old days, media plans were put together using simple spreadsheets with columns clearly marked for "print," "radio," and "broadcast

TV." Media choices were limited, the rules (reach and frequency) were well established, and decision-making lead times were long. Today, strategic media buying means dealing with volatility and unpredictability, and it requires the ability to manage media dynamically, in real time.

Media planning, once the weak stepchild to Creativity, is now assuming its proper place among agency priorities. But planning for targeted media channels is much more difficult—and more expensive—than planning for untargeted channels with broad reach.

New digital channels are appearing and evolving with breathtaking speed. They now include search marketing, contextual media, behavioral image/text ads, podcasting, video, rich media, mobile, digital billboard, digital radio, and even advertising on time-shifting devices such as TiVo. Some of them, including search advertising, have established rules, but, from a traditional media planning perspective, these new rules are odd and almost counterintuitive. Other platforms, including mobile advertising, are still in the experimental stage, and yet few doubt that in the coming years they all will become an increasingly important element in the media planner's playbook.

Query or search-based advertising, because it times and tunes marketing messages and then serves those highly relevant messages dynamically according to the context in which they are requested, is likely to be a major part of any new platform emerging from the ranks of digital media marketing. In addition to search advertising, there is also contextual keyword-targeted advertising as well as the behaviorally targeted ads, which leave an even more powerful impression. But the actual advertising opportunities differ markedly on each new digital platform, and so do the form and content of advertising designed for them. What these platforms all share is that they will be "smart," which means they will be able to sense the context in which advertising appears as well as the individual viewing that content. Individual behavioral profiles may contain personally identifiable information (if the consumer opted in) or may simply contain a wealth of nonpersonally identifiable historical information that can assist in targeting advertising.

Each of these new channels presents a major challenge to Madison Avenue's old school media planners, who traditionally have budgeted money in simple spreadsheets allocated to print, TV, radio, etc. Simply adding "online" to their canonical spreadsheets is not enough because "online" now includes such a broad range of applications and targeting parameters.

The marketing possibilities of each of these insurgent channels cannot profitably be exploited without understanding what these possibilities are, what the advertising potentials are for each of them, and how to buy media on them. All too often marketers are badly served by their agencies, which produce media plans that look backward to last year's plan instead of looking to the much more complex and challenging media environment that lies ahead.

Advertising agencies need to accelerate their operations in order to recognize that the world is living according to accelerated Internet time. It is no longer acceptable for media plans to be locked in on a year-by-year basis. Uncertainty needs to be institutionalized into the planning process.

Agencies also need to adjust their financial operations to take account of this new dynamic media marketplace. Traditionally, agencies made their money on the 15 percent net/gross spread on their media invoices. Even when the client/advertiser negotiated a lower rate for media, commissions rarely departed from the 15 percent markup. Over the years clients negotiated media commissions far lower than 15 percent, pushing agencies to keep media and account teams lean and institutionalizing the simplified media plan. Agencies are expected to volunteer more complex and targeted media plans with their commissions cut way down, but auctions run by Google, Yahoo, and Microsoft are based on net cost. Those invoices are produced with just one number (the net cost, typically a CPC or CPM), which means that in effect, agencies must "gross up" the media, highlighting the agency fees every time the marketer pays the bills.

Advertising firms need to develop an approach to media management that is instantly responsive to an ever-changing dynamic environment. Increasingly, digital media management happens in real time, and the results learned today must be analyzed and transformed into actionable processes that can be used to design and execute campaigns that will work better tomorrow. This process of continual optimization requires continual experimentation, testing, and a feedback process that is not part of the old analog media management model. Even media that isn't managed in real time must be optimized with increasing frequency.

3.2 New Methods of Valuing Advertising

Broadly targeted banner and display advertising, whether charged by impression or by slotting fee for time-period sponsorship, will likely remain an important component in the digital marketer's arsenal as many advertisers will always have situations where it makes sense to get their message in front of as many people as possible, regardless of the cost or the wasted impressions. There will always be marketers with enough cash to make such expenditures, just as there will be marketers who don't care about performance, regardless of whether it is measured through traditional direct response metrics including, ROI, ROAS, CPA (cost per acquisition) or branding success metrics including purchase intent, recall, and awareness.

But in the past few years, advertisers have embraced performance-based advertising and, consequently, it has grown to be a significantly more important form of digital marketing. Performance-based advertising works by targeting current technologies that allow the marketer to know enough about the user doing the "performing" to in turn allow publishers to earn higher yields. Of course, All clicks are not equal, and users in-market for a particular good or service are worth much more to marketers than those who are not. But being able to know as much as possible about the user, including performance/click history, demographics, and other background data, allows marketers to pay variable amounts for different users based upon their unique qualities.

For those marketers who do care about things such as efficiency, targeted traffic, ROI, and smart marketing, the key to successful digital marketing is the ability to distinguish individuals, serve each of them ads that are most likely to produce a successful result, and pay an appropriate price for each exposure or click. The technology required to accomplish this goal is comparatively new, but this function is the most important differentiator of digital marketing from its analog

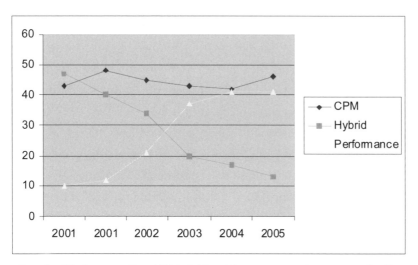

Growth of Performance-Based Digital Advertising 2000–2005 (percentage of online ad spend). Source: IAB (Note: The designation "Hybrid" refers to mixed-model advertising involving both a CPM and a performance componen.t)

predecessors. Such technology can make banner ads, text ads, and any future form of digital marketing more valuable to all marketing stake-holders, including the advertiser, publisher, and consumer. Typically, because its value varies widely depending on the context of its exposure, performance-based advertising is not purchased in the traditional way. Increasingly, we are seeing media sold using an auction mechanism, which presents unique challenges that require a whole new way of thinking about and buying media. Currently, search clicks are the largest share of the online performance media spend, but we can expect these auction marketplaces to continue to grow.

3.3 From Silo'd to Integrated Marketing

The arbitrary division of the traditional agency structure into "above the line" and "below the line" divisions may have made some sense in the era when most money was spent on network buys. But in the current marketing environment, it makes no sense whatsoever, especially when considering the growth of these expenditures in the overall ad mix.

In July 2006, the Winterberry Group studied the advertising industry, specifically assessing the new requirements imposed on agencies by the emerging digital marketing environment. Among its findings was that "the complex demands of the multi-channel selling environment require that agencies provide clients with a unified offering spanning both 'above the-line' and 'below-the-line' marketing channels." Unfortunately, the study found that traditional advertising agencies are often structurally incapable of accommodating integrated marketing objectives: "Traditionally, most agencies chose to isolate these channels in the broader marketing plan, effectively treating them as supplementary to the highly-visual branding campaign."

That below-the-line (BTL) spending is occupying a greater share of the overall marketing services budget illustrates the evolution of adver-

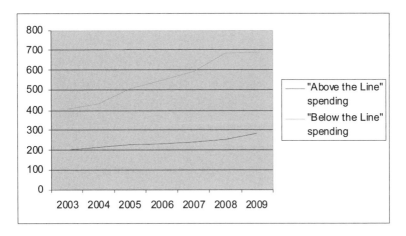

Above-the-Line vs. Below-the-Line Spending (in billions). Source: V12 and the
Winterberry Group, 2006, as republished in OMMA Magazine, August 2006.

tising beyond the traditional paradigm of thirty-second-spot and
untargeted media buy. It also underscores the importance of marketers
being able to understand and integrate multiplatform advertising
efforts that occur across a range of media channels. The promise of
digital media is that for the first time it gives marketers the potential of
complete insight into how advertising works, how messages are consumed, and how customers respond to them. When used with appropriate targeting technologies, advertising can be made more relevant to
the life of each individual consumer it touches, eliminating the obtru-
siveness associated with traditional advertising methods.

The rise of BTL spending requires that agencies think more holistically about the media ecosystem and apply concentrated effort to opti-
mizing each media channel's contribution to the overall marketing
mix. As the notion of the general-purpose practitioner has yielded to
the specialist in the practice of medicine, the all-purpose general ad
agency is similarly passing by the wayside. Specialists with expertise in
media buying, digital media, search media, and other below-the-line

marketing disciplines will grow increasingly important in this new world, and although it is possible to assemble such a team of specialists within one organization, clients will need to be convinced that the value of such bundled services far outweighs the alternative of each specialist competing separately for the client's business.

Because the execution of these tasks has been so complicated by the entry of digital marketing onto the scene, however, most advertisers will continue to outsource the tasks performed by an advertising agency to an external intermediary. Whether the realization of high-level marketing goals is measured in ROI, ROAS, or brand metrics including the recently fashionable "engagement," these goals will need to be translated into a myriad of small decisions in order to be executed in a way that achieves realization. Regardless of whether all media is being managed by one agency or several specialist firms, it is the marketer's responsibility to understand how various segments of the marketing and media plan might interact. Even as increased targeting allows marketers to pay for a portion of their media on a performance basis, an integrated plan relies on more than just immediately observable direct-response metrics.

3.4 From Manual to Automated Media Exchanges

There have been numerous attempts to provide alternatives to Madison Avenue's archaic, manually driven systems. A few of them, launched during the go-go 1990s, actually gathered some traction, but none survived the dot-com meltdown. This meltdown was unfortunate, but the stifling of many good ideas was a likely result of the unrealistically aggressive financial demands of venture capitalists of the era in tandem with the inability of those solutions to gain critical mass due to industry inertia.

The present ad industry lags behind its clients in technology

Screenshot from AdAuction.com, an Early Automated Media Exchange Site

prowess. Today, a tremendous amount of energy is still being expended to simply establish whether a given ad ran at a given time. The auditing process, in addition to all functions related to billing and reconciliation, are in critical need of the kind of streamlining that has been commonplace among the ad industry's client base for many years.

Media delivery systems are increasingly adding digital trafficking, production, and delivery mechanisms. Such media now include radio, TV, print, Internet, outdoor, IP TV, podcasts, XM/Sirius, TiVo, custom printing, and mobile. Thus, developing a set of data standards may result in either a central place for marketers and network owners to buy and sell media or simply a framework by which technology can centralize the research, buying reporting, and reconciliation required by the differing needs of marketers.

Automated exchanges occur in a dynamic environment in which the value of any given ad unit, combination of ad units, or campaign is either arranged in a traditional one-to-one negotiated process or determined by the market in an auction. The advantage of auction-based media exchanges is the elimination of friction in the buying process. This term "friction," applied by economists to markets, marketplaces, and economic systems, relates to inefficiencies within a marketplace that result in mispricing of the assets traded, bought, or sold in the market. Eliminating friction increases market efficiency.

In the stock market, many laws regarding insider trading, disclosure of material information about publicly traded companies, and accounting statement accuracy are in place in order to maintain an efficient and fair flow of information. Similarly, commodities are sold in an open marketplace because sellers believe it results in the highest commodity prices. By commodifying valuable media, the digital marketplace has proven that it can also be auctioned for a high price. These automated auction systems, which began with search marketing, are being deployed for increasing amounts of online inventory. Aside from search, the most common online advertising to be auctioned are channel-based text, or banner placements; contextually targeted text, or banner ads; and behaviorally targeted inventory. Though auction billing methods such as CPA, CPC, and CPM may differ, auction-based, automated management systems all have one thing in common: they are designed to maximize publisher and network profit while marketers fight for the valuable consumers in an auction. Network targeting and ad-serving systems, such as Google's AdSense, calculate in almost real time the highest predicted yield among all the ads in a large database, and then serve those ads. In order for any media marketplace to succeed, the consumers being targeted must be valuable. If the advertising inventory is not valued by marketers, the clearing price of the auction will be low, and this very lack of highly valuable eyeballs was the downfall of many of the early online and offline media marketplaces. Likewise, lack of a common and agreed-upon set of methods of valuation for these eyeballs results in uncertainty and advertiser paralysis. Thus the marketplace fails.

For publishers and media owners, automated media exchanges that contain properly described media assets provide tangible benefits. Currently, other than the PPC search-media exchanges, most automated media exchanges and marketplaces provide a way for underutilized nonpremium media inventory (often referred to as "remnant" inventory) to be more easily sold. While each item (impression or other advertising unit) in such inventory may not have much inherent value individually, when aggregated and segmented, this "long tail" of inventory acquires value that would otherwise not exist.

Because they eliminate inefficiencies associated with traditional media buying practices, thereby lowering administrative costs, such automated exchanges realize enormous potential benefits for advertisers. Auction-based exchanges allow the market—not individual buyers and sellers—to determine the value of any given advertising unit, thus equalizing the power disparities that have existed in media markets (such as broadcasting) where one party (the broadcasters) has traditionally enjoyed bargaining advantage due to its knowledge of inventory levels and the lack of pricing transparency.

Automated systems have the potential of letting advertisers design, monitor, and execute smarter media plans that take maximal advantage of opportunities that would otherwise not be visible. In the same way, network owners have more options to monetize inventory that would otherwise be unsellable—for example, airtime that was cancelled at the last moment.

The fact that advertising lacks an automated system of exchanging intelligence about media opportunities is not a theoretical problem, but rather one that is very real and has obstructed advertising's evolution from a wasteful to an efficient marketing mechanism. According to a 2004 Forrester report, what is really holding back the advent of more advanced targeting in the cable television industry is not the lack of appropriate technology, but rather the persistence of archaic media buying and trafficking methods: "Geographic targeting by cable zone [a neighborhood of 2,000 to 80,000 homes] is technically possible using spot [local] cable, but the manual, high-overhead nature of the media buying and trafficking process makes this impractical to do with any scale and complexity." (What's Next For TV Advertising, Forrester Research, 12/23/04). Again, the failure of the buy-side of the industry to take advantage of the additional targeting options already available results in less relevant local advertising that tends to be ignored by the viewer.

3.5 Erosion of "Upfront" Media Buying

There is no greater indicator of Madison Avenue's deplorable backwardness than its annual "Upfronts." This ritual began in the early 1960s when ABC, the weakest network, made the decision to launch its new shows in the week following Labor Day. After CBS and NBC followed suit, the Upfront became a tradition. So each year in May, ad agency and broadcast reps gather in New York at a weeklong ceremony filled with glitz and glamour. Broadcast owners put on lavish shows, hype the hot shows debuting that fall, and try to lock in as many airtime bookings possible for the maximum price allowed. Media buyers representing major airtime buyers try to negotiate the best possible price for this valuable airtime, And many of these negotiating sessions last all night as buyers and sellers attempt to hammer out their differences. Billions of dollars change hands in a single week, long before anyone can answer the most obvious of questions: will people actually watch any of this programming?

Advertisers had grumbled about the Upfronts for a long time. As early as 1970, after broadcasters raised CPM prices by more than 20 percent, J. Walter Thompson pulled out of the Upfront (Jack Meyers Report). And in the mid 1980s, the networks reacted to the encroaching reach of the cable networks not by lowering prices, but rather by increasing the number of minutes available for commercial bookings. By 2004, the unhappiness was palpable: when the Association of National Advertisers polled its members about how well the Upfront was working for them, 58 percent reported being dissatisfied, with only 4 percent reporting being "very satisfied." Only 27 percent of advertisers reported that they believed the process had any value. (MediaPost, May 2004, http://publications.mediapost.com/index.cfm?fuseaction=Articles.show Article&art_aid=4455)

But the imbalance of supply and demand kept the Upfront going: as long as advertisers were willing to lay out huge chunks of money to buy what were essentially "media futures," broadcasters could basically dictate terms, and they milked this opportunity for all it was worth. In the last few years, however, the institution of the Upfront has begun to show some real cracks, and this erosion is due to the declining effectiveness of untargeted broadcasting. In early 2004, a group of advertisers and agencies formed an organization called the Network Upfront Discussion Group (NUDG). Its purposes were modest: to move the Upfront, which traditionally happened in May, closer to the actual beginning of the fall TV season, which begins each September, and to institute a "closing bell" that would end the traditional madness of the Upfronts. Although NUDG' purposes were unrealized, it did signal a new mood in the air that indicated a need to take power back from the networks in order to level the advertising playing field .

By the time of the 2005 Upfronts, however, the mood among advertisers had soured completely. In a poll of marketers taken by the ANA and Advertising Age, 69 percent of marketers surveyed reported that they would be buying less network TV, with only 5 percent saying they wanted to buy more (ANA/AdAge Survey, 2004). Tapping into this unhappiness, an insurgent group of advertisers—led by Wal-Mart, Hewlett-Packard, Masterfoods, Microsoft, Philips, and Toyota—announced that it would build, on its own, an electronic marketplace to serve as an alternative to the broadcasting establishment's annual Upfront media buying frenzy period, in which billions of dollars' worth of ad bookings were placed for shows beginning the next September. Ebay was the winner in the bid to build the "E-Media Exchange."

The "Upfront Insurgent's" plan for the E-Media Exchange was bold, audacious, and fundamentally straightforward. It specified that the process of buying and selling advertising would work in the way that Initial Public Offerings (IPOs) of stocks are floated in the stock exchange. Networks would offer spots with an initial value and, using an electronic trading system, prices would ebb and flow with demand. If there was insufficient demand for a given spot, it could be bought back by the network and then added to the pool of spots available for later purchase in the "scatter" market.

If fully implemented, the benefits of the E-Media Exchange included the elimination of inefficiencies associated with the manually negotiated, fax and phone order way of buying and selling media. Most important, an auction would eliminate the widespread practice employed by broadcast networks that forced marketers to buy time in bundles: in order to buy air time on good, top-rated shows, marketers had to also buy air time on bad, bottom-rated shows. But an auction would eliminate bundling and let the value of poorly performing programming be set by the market at lower rates.

Naturally, this idea didn't please the network owners. In fact, they were practically apoplectic, with all but one deciding to boycott any such exchange. After all, letting the market establish the value of their programming might cause them to lose money. Their reaction was immediate and furious. One network president said it was "ridiculous

. . . we'll never do that. That commoditizes your product."(Media Post article: 7/706). Other broadcasters quietly let it be known that they would boycott the E-Media Exchange due to the obvious fear that it would cut their prices. Even Wall Street got into the game: one analyst recommended that the E-Media Exchange, while a minor threat, should be closely watched because, if it caught on, it would cause a decline in broadcast valuations. Still, the project chugged along and, suddenly, the words "auction media" seemed to be on every ad man's lips.

While this battle between the insurgents and the networks was raging, Johnson & Johnson, which spends more than $1 billion dollars a year for all of their advertising, simply walked away from the Upfront. Shortly afterward, it announced its intention to shift 20 percent of its budget into media that promised to offer more accountable metrics.

The networks could fume, but ultimately the advertisers had the power to vote, and they were voting by withholding dollars.

3.6 Will Marketers Actually Buy Media This Way?

While Automated Media Marketplaces (AMMs) have long-term promise, it is unlikely that they will replace all forms of media buying anytime soon. Instead, they will first appear as an adjunct to the old, negotiated model, and they will be specifically applied to the most undesirable media available in any given channel. In other words, they will be used to monetize inventory whose value is either low or unable to be currently quantified. Such inventory is traditionally referred to as "distressed" or "remnant" media, and it could be said to comprise a "long tail" of advertising opportunities, none of which have a high enough value on their own to warrant spending the overhead costs on arranging a purchase. Automated exchanges, however, allow media buys to occur so economically that such inventory acquires a value that it did not have before.

There are limits to how much inventory can be sold in this way. This is because the whole idea behind an auction is predicated on two things: scarcity and a mechanism with a sufficiently limited number of variables controlling who wins and who loses. A rare painting or other one-of-a-kind work of art is a perfect candidate for an auction: there's only one painting, and if you have more than one person who wants to buy that painting, you have the makings of an auction. The same is true in search marketing: positions on SERPS (Search Engine Results Pages) are finite, and lots of people want to own these positions. One does find scarcity in the broadcast market: only one advertiser can appear in a given time slot running on a prime-time TV or radio show.

But some forms of media do not lend themselves to the auction process because scarcity does not exist. One example of this is print advertising. While it might make sense to create an auction for pre-ferred positions (e.g., placement on the inside or outside cover page), auctions function best when the commodity in question is scarce (e.g., a position on a SERP or an original work of art). Because a newspaper or magazine can simply print additional pages, auctions for print advertising have hitherto been unsuccessful, and it is not likely that these positions will be sold this way in the future.

There's another, less obvious, issue with auction-based media exchanges that will likely limit their attractiveness to marketers. Even if enough media owners come forward to provide an inventory of good media opportunities, a critical question remains: will advertisers, who really have the power (because they have the money) be more comfort-able buying inventory through auction rather than negotiation? How much more were advertisers really willing to pay to "lock in" advertis-ing positions in advance?

This question is important because of the influence that big buyers of media exert on the media-buying process. Proctor & Gamble, for example, buys approximately one third of all television advertising. For this giant manufacturer, being able to lock in large parcels of airtime in advance and at a fixed price lets it know exactly how much a given campaign will cost. And advertisers like P&G don't just buy electronic media; they buy billboards, sponsorships, store end-caps, and other offline media. These multichannel, multimodal campaigns consist of a tremendous number of individual elements, all of which must function together in a way much like the parts of a well-oiled machine. Nothing can be left to chance.

Uncertainty, in other words, is anathema to the way that large advertisers think, and it is precisely this uncertainty that auctions introduce. Not only is the final price of an item uncertain at the onset of any given auction, but so is the identity of the winner. Although the odds are small that a giant such as P&G, charged with the awesome responsibility of moving 20 million diapers in a couple of weeks, might be denied a critical component of a complex media plan because a smaller diaper manufacturer outbid it, the existence of this mere chance is not just unthinkable: it's practically obscene.

Additionally, because auctions work best in environments with very few and very simple variables, the buying and selling of advertising media presents a challenge to the auction format. For example, in the search-marketing environment, the main variables are click price, which influences position, and creativity, which occurs within the tightly constrained text character limit required by the engines. But in the traditional media environment, the variables are much more complex. For example, repetition is critical for influencing buyer behavior; the general rule is that between three and five impressions are necessary before the potential buyer does anything. In this environment, advertisers are paying as much for the guarantee that their spots will run where and when specified as they are for the value of the actual airtime. Unless the E-Media Exchange offers the ability to auction not just individual spot positions, but entire campaigns, appeal will be limited.

Interestingly, on the other hand, the broadcasters likely underestimate the power of an auction-media exchange. If all broadcast inventory were to make it into the Exchange, economists argue that the prices paid on high-value inventory might rise dramatically, thus balancing out any rate depression. Media buyers would therefore still be paying for bundles of airtime based on a blended value, mixing the great with the good and the bad.

The Media Buyer's Guide to Auction-Based Advertising

If you are at an agency or are an in-house media planner/buyer, chances are you've added search-engine marketing, the first widely successful auction-driven form of advertising, to your online plans. As a cutting-edge media buyer, you approach search marketing from a unique perspective, defining search traffic as media. Search has special characteristics that may strike more traditional media buyers are very odd. Here are some of them:

Limited inventory. With search media, inventory is fixed, as with TV ads during the Super Bowl. Only a certain number of people search for a given keyword or phrase every day at the major search portals.

Inverse volume discounts. A consequence of limited inventory is a really crazy phenomenon (until you get used to it). Let's say a $5,000, monthlong test worked. Your cost-per-order (CPO)/cost-per-action (CPA) or branding metrics were met, and the client is ecstatic. Now, you want more. The budget is increased to $20,000 a month, but the inventory may not even exist. And if it does, it will cost you per click, as you displace advertisers who pay more in auction-style engines.

Limited negotiation. You can't negotiate in an auction. Because of the dynamic aspect of this marketplace, it's important that your objectives are mapped out clearly. Objectives can be position, click volume, or CPC averages/caps.

Unpredictable budget and click volume. A biggie for those accustomed to knowing exactly what a spend or click volume will be within media buys. How much should you allocate toward search if you're new to the game? Getting a fix on this question is very difficult.

Search, the first real advertising-on-demand medium, is morphing beyond the desktop-browser paradigm. But wherever it goes, these unusual features will shape the advertising market it creates.

Solutions: How Do You Plan for the Unplannable?

Digital media, unlike its analog predecessors, is inherently protean. In the old days, things moved slowly. It took decades for media capabilities and media consumption patterns to change, and lead times for buying and selling media were measured in months. By correctly assessing the tactical environment and placing a few bets among a few different channels, you'd be okay.

Then, the language of media buying was simpler. Metrics such as reach and frequency were easy to understand and prices changed incrementally, perhaps once a year, when publishers and network owners adjusted their CPMs. But today, pricing models are shifting to auction-based, dynamic pricing models that are both complicated and difficult to budget for. In effect, the world of traditional media is moving beyond the world of the fixed media plan and the fixed budget into an era in which advertising expenses need to be continually monitored and ad campaigns need to be continually refined. Doing this will require a new way of thinking about buying media.

3.7 Solutions: Build a Media Slush Fund

The term "slush fund" is attached to some unfortunate connotations. Traditionally, slush funds have been used by corrupt politicians to finance bribes and conduct other underhanded transactions, but in marketing there should be a different kind of slush fund: a discretionary account that you have at your disposal that doesn't have go through a lengthy approval process. Think of this kind of slush fund as a sum of money that is set aside for yet-to-be-decided purposes. Such funds allow the flexibility to inject money into new media projects that are so new that their success metrics may not yet be established.

From a marketing perspective, there are many forms of media that qualify as purely experimental. These include satellite radio, HD radio, podcasting, mobile marketing, and other forms too new to have yet established their worth. And, as digital media forms continue to proliferate and morph, they will certainly continue to be joined by others in the future. The search engines are exerting enormous pressure to add such media inventory.

Here's the exciting part: media that is too new to be measurable is defined by the advertising establishment as "nonpremium," "distressed," or "remnant." This means that it's undervalued, and also that there will be very few players investing in it. The chances are high that you can obtain high visibility without paying a premium, at least until such time that this new media is discovered by slower-footed marketers.

Will you be the first marketer or the last to define and seize the marketing possibilities of these new forms? Well, you'll never have an easy time arguing the merits of an unproven media form to those for whom success potential needs to be demonstrated in advance and, by the time you win the argument, you'll have missed the opportunity. Hence the necessity of having a slush fund that you control in order to fund an experimental spend.

Think of new media slush funds the same way you think about Research and Development. The dollars that you put into R&D may not pay back tomorrow: in fact, the odds are that most of these projects will *never* pay off. But if you happen to be the first to be able to exploit a new digital marketing medium, because you'll be among a select few who understand how to make this medium work, the lessons learned may be invaluable. Even though the majority of projects you invest in may not provide enough positive ROI to justify continued investment, the one that is in fact a winner may justify all the failed experiments.

If you have experience in direct marketing or other below the line marketing disciplines, you're probably comfortable thinking about media spending in this way. Testing, experimentation, and feedback are part of your culture, and these skills are highly applicable to all forms of digital media which will emerge. But if you come from the more traditional world where media spend is determined in advance, it may take some selling on your part before your budget masters give you the freedom you need to research and develop an approach to emergent media.

3.8 Solutions: Build a Nimble Team

There are definitely distinct traits that favor nimble organizations over sclerotic ones when attempting to manage developments in dynamic media environments. One of the most important is the number of decision points intervening between the process of decision making and an action. The fewer the number, the greater the speed of responsiveness, and thus better the organization's ability to adapt quickly to a fast-changing environment.

The degree to which authority is delegated is an important determinant of a given organization's ability to respond. If each and every decision must be vetted and approved by a superior, this will inhibit the overall responsiveness of any team. Wherever possible, arbitrary hierarchies should be flattened, and creative individuals should be encouraged to enjoy as much power as they require to accomplish their goals.

Nothing in the above paragraph will be news to anyone who has ever tried to build a responsive organization. In fact, these principles date back at least half a century. The fact that most businesses are not able to implement them says as much about human nature as it does about the way businesses must be organized. Change, despite popular lip service, isn't something that's welcomed by most people, and it is especially poorly welcomed by those who have earned their positions of power through years of doing their jobs a certain way. This is why self-described "change agents" often get themselves thrown out of their organizations within a few months after being hired specifically to make changes.

But change, thanks to the Internet and its enabled processes, is something that will happen to any organization, regardless of the degree to which individual stakeholders actively resist it. It is not a matter of "if" but of "when," and this change is happening sooner than many like it.

Digital marketing today requires a unique blend of skills not taught in business schools or learned in old-line ad agencies. Finding people who are both creative and quantitatively minded enough to work effectively in this new environment is difficult. And because you will likely spend time and resources training them, it's imperative to hold on to them. Unlike the dot-com era, in which many people were lured into staying through the offering of stock options, today's environment requires that these employees are rewarded in the here and now, by paying them competitively and treating them humanely.

Make sure your people have the freedom to explore new roles, learn new ways of doing things, and have enough bandwidth to investigate over-the-horizon marketing technologies that, although they may represent tiny fragments of your present business now, may grow to large chunks tomorrow. Get them to conferences, symposia, and hooked into thought circles discussing the future of search and other emerging auction-based media. Create an environment that encourages independent thought, debate, and dialogue. Google does this, and they do so because they know the next multibillion-dollar market may result from some "cool" gizmo that one of their people creates on her free time.

You probably can't go as far as Google does in terms of providing a rich, almost university-like environment for your people to work in, but you still need to invest in your staff if you want to keep them. Think of your staff the same way you think of your customers: as crucial stakeholders in your enterprise's future. Remember, you can have a great client base and the greatest technology in the world today, but it's ultimately your "wetware"—the people with the expertise to use all of your assets in order to maximize your clients' return on their investment in search—that will provide your strongest and most sustaining competitive advantage tomorrow.

3.9 Solutions: Don't Fall in Love with Your Media Plan

New forms of digital media are emerging so quickly that it is said that marketers live in an age of permanent "media emergency." A clear example of this is the remarkable ascension of YouTube.com from almost nothing into a marketing platform holding enough potential to justify Google's purchase of it in 2006 for more than $1.5 billion. Other examples include Myspace.com, acquired by Fox Interactive, Flickr, Deli.cio.us, and others. Currently, there are many bets being placed on these new platforms providing new and compelling marketing opportunities, but the only ones who understand their potential worth are those doing the experimenting.

When confronted with such unexpected media emergences, the traditional approach has been to wait until the media has established itself as effective, perform an appropriate valuation of its worth, staff a team with expertise in its unique features, plan a test campaign, and dip one's toes in over a reasonable period of time. Only after an appropriate evaluation period has passed can judgment be passed on a given media's potential. The problem with this approach is that, by the time a team is built, staffed, and trained, it may be too late to fully utilize it.

Those who first exploited the potentialities of search-engine marketing were surprised and amazed by how well it worked. Many enjoyed reasonable keyword prices and very profitable marketing campaigns, but quickly learned that the absence of effective barriers to entry into search-engine marketing also meant that their advantage was quickly lost. As competitors entered the market, higher keyword costs were imposed and, for some, the necessity to invest in automation systems and dedicated staffs to run their campaigns became crucial. What had seemed a very easy way to build market share and ROI very quickly proved to be a much more daunting environment than was initially anticipated. Additionally, as the search engines are constantly changing their ad-serving algorithms, it's no wonder marketers have expressed surprise and disappointment at what initially seemed an easy, economical marketing medium.

But one important revelation these early search-engine marketers had was the need to embrace a multiplatform approach to search marketing. When considered along with their distribution partners, different search engines provide markedly different audiences that need to be addressed in different ways, including an understanding of each one's unique targeting capabilities. The principles of Media and Marketing 101 continue to apply in this new world: always buy your best media first, on whichever combination of platform/channel/engine providing it. The problem, however, is that achieving this goal imposes a considerable overhead on the marketer. Search campaigns are not interchangeable among engines: each must be constructed individually and monitored independently. For large campaigns, this can entail an extensive and often unanticipated expenditure of time and effort, which is one of the reasons marketers running sophisticated campaigns outsource this task to a specialized agency with the tools to manage multiplatform efforts.

CHAPTER 4

Lyin' Eyes

The New Search Engine
and Digital Media Marketplaces are
Neither Fair nor Transparent

"Why can't advertisers know from the start what Google allows?"

—Danny Sullivan, Search Engine Watch, 9/22/04,
http://searchenginewatch.com/showPage.html?page=3411111

*

THE MARKETPLACE that Google and the other engines have introduced is full of potential for marketers, but it's also full of traps. These hazards aren't always obvious, and they are rarely discussed at New Media, Interactive, or Search conferences or by industry analysts. Call them the ugly little secrets of the business: the stuff you see only after you've bought millions of dollars of clicks on behalf of hundreds of customers; the stuff you learn only after you've been around the block a couple of times and talked to enough people who've been beaten up in this market.

The new digital media marketplaces pioneered by search engines are less than transparent. In fact, these easy-to-use, self-service ad platforms conceal a myriad of pitfalls and traps that defy the notion that the digital media marketplace is fair and transparent. Finding ways around these hidden traps poses new burdens and headaches for marketers, and understanding how to maximize profit in a partially opaque real-time media marketplace is an art and a science.

The power that the targeted digital-media marketplaces created by the search engines has bestowed on advertisers is unprecedented. Never in the history of marketing have we been given such an efficient, flexible, accountable, and nonobtrusive marketing channel. Never before have so many marketers been able to use this channel to achieve strategic business objectives. Yet at the same time search marketing can be hazardous, unrewarding, infinitely frustrating, and financially unprofitable as CPCs rise. The mere fact that we've been given new powers doesn't mean they will be used wisely. In fact, because the process of managing search campaigns is so inherently complex, many marketers will likely enter the market unprepared and unequipped to deal with its tougher, more maddening aspects.

4.1 What the Search Engines Won't Tell You

Many marketers believe the search engines should be doing more to protect us from these harsher realities. Google and the other engines are all too willing to sell clicks and, although they've generally done a good job in providing detailed recommendations as to how to run profitable campaigns, they're naturally disinclined to provide much information that might dissuade novice marketers from buying clicks that are not at all likely to result in conversions. After all, their business is to sell marketers clicks, not conversions. However, the long-term viability of the PPC search marketplace requires marketers to understand the true value of the search clicks they are buying and pay a price with a positive marginal profit contribution.

Perhaps we're dreaming, but I'd like to see Google, Yahoo, Microsoft, and the other engines run a big, flashing, neon-colored warning sign that would appear before any marketer was allowed to hit the "Start Campaign" button. Here's what we'd like to see on this sign:

Welcome to the wonderful world of search marketing! Before you begin your search campaign, and before we start the highly pleasurable process (at least to us) of taking the lion's share of your marketing dollars, please acknowledge that you have read and fully understand the following points, to wit:

1. We, your favorite search engine, bear absolutely no responsibility for the success of your search-marketing campaign. To be absolutely frank with you, other than the negative PR we get when your campaign fails and you complain to the press, it makes no difference to us whether you're making or losing money, just as long as you continue to buy clicks from us. Please don't come back to us in a month—or at any time in the future—complaining that you've spent a lot of money and have gotten squat in return. The fact that you are only launching a search campaign now while your competition have been honing their keywords, copy, landing pages, and offers for several years proves you just don't get it. Therefore, your ability to catch up to your competition and run a profitable campaign is unlikely. Don't ask us for help. We're far too busy creating cool gizmos to be bothered with your campaign's problems, which, after all, are your responsibility, not ours. If we are going to help any marketers, it's going to be the ones who already understand this market and have been paying us millions for several years. Those marketers are fairly low maintenance.

2. The search marketplace is auction-based, dynamic, hyper-competitive, and opaque. You may *think* you know what you're going to pay for any given click, but we reserve the right to change the rules on you at any time, using our patented, highly secret and complicated algorithms that even a rocket scientist would have difficulty explaining. If you don't like the way we run this market, we welcome you to choose one of the other engines, but frankly, we're all running black-box-driven opaque marketplaces, so you might as well stick with us and try to make it work.

3. We, your favorite search engine, are proud to offer a range of highly sophisticated, laserlike targeting technologies, including geo-targeting, demographic targeting, dayparting, and (soon) behavioral targeting. These tools can give you an edge whenever you run into a competitor who's decided to systematically outspend you for the top paid search placements (which will happen more frequently than you'd like). We suggest you employ these tools whenever possible, but before you start using them be aware that even a single keyword can now have thousands of permutations. So before turning these power-ful tools on, get used to the idea that you'll be spending the rest of your mortal days in front of your computer, continually tweaking these targeted micro-channels to provide maximum ROI.

4. For most of your keywords we already have tens or hundreds of advertisers. There are two kinds of advertisers at the top of the results:

    A. Brilliant marketers running highly relevant ads that have been crafted through expensive trial and error.

    B. Clueless idiots who simply throw more and more money at our system, elbowing their way into top position while over-paying for clicks.

We're not losing any sleep waiting for any of the engines to provide this kind of warning statement. We do hope, however, that more mar-keters realize how treacherous and rocky the road to sustainable prof-itability is before they hit the "Start Campaign" button. Taking account of the steep challenges is the first step toward bracing yourself for suc-cess in the search marketplace, and the more prepared you are, the bet-ter you'll fare as the search marketing continues to evolve.

4.2 Your Money Isn't Good Enough

Despite the promise the Internet has made to provide transparency to marketers, there are hidden factors that make auction-based media marketplaces work in ways that are neither fully transparent nor fair. Let's think about the way a normal auction works and then compare it to the way an auction run by Google or another hybrid auction works (note: all of the search engines, including those run by Yahoo and Microsoft, are now hybrids). Let's think about the most straightforward auction you can imagine: an auction of a painting at Christie's. At the appointed time, the painting is brought on stage, set up on an easel, and the bidding begins. Bidders come forward, state prices, and the one who bids the highest price before the drop of the gavel gets to take the painting home. For purposes of this example, let's say the winning bid on this painting is $100,000.

Now imagine the exact same scenario, with one crucial modification. Before the high bidder hands over the money and takes the painting home, the auctioneer asks him a series of questions. Where will the painting go? How will it be transported? How will it be hung? By whom? After marking down the answers to these questions, and after checking whether the answers agree with the auction house's guidelines, the auctioneer takes out a small pocket calculator, performs a series of calculations, prints out a small piece of paper, and hands it to the high bidder.

"$125,000?" asks the incredulous bidder. "I thought I was paying $100,000!"

"According to our guidelines," intones the auctioneer, "which exist to protect the auction house, the users of the auction house, and auctions generally, you must pay a $25,000 premium."

"But I can only afford $100,000" says the high bidder.

"Please step aside, sir, so that the auction may continue," says the auctioneer, eyeing the burly bouncers standing on both sides of the painting.

A few minutes later, someone else bids $100,000, and again, the auctioneer asks his questions of the bidder. After the new calculations are performed, this new high bidder gets to take the painting home. As he is taking the painting out of the auction room, the first high bidder asks him a question.

"How much did you pay?"

"$90,000" replies the painting's new owner.

"How can that be possible?" asks the aggrieved first high bidder.

"I buy a lot of paintings here, and they know my paintings will be hung professionally in relevant areas of my gallery so I guess they like me." replies the owner.

"But this is an auction!" protests the first high bidder.

"Sort of," replies the owner, rolling the painting away on a dolly.

You might think this scenario is crazy, which it would be if it happened in a real auction house like Christie's. In fact, if Christie's did this sort of thing, they'd probably be investigated by the Federal Trade Commission for unfair and discriminatory trade practices.

But exactly the same thing happens thousands of times a minute on Google, Yahoo, and Microsoft's adCenter (as well as on the other engines) because they don't look exclusively at bid prices but also use predicted click-through-rates that favor marketers who have built a brand online and tend buy a lot of clicks, and penalizes those who don't buy as many. Like the auctioneer in the above example, the engines reason that their tilted playing field is justified by the greater purpose served by making their displayed results more relevant. But marketers who've actually experienced this kind of price discrimination feel aggrieved and, in our view, they have a right to, even though the engines also have a right to maximize their effective yield by looking at predicted click-through-rates, not just CPC bid.

This strange aspect of the search-auction market—that some buyers pay much more than others for the same position on a SERP—has another unusual dimension. It usually works in favor of large, branded marketers and against marketers who are small or unknown. This is because users of search engines are more likely to click on text ads mentioning brands they have already been exposed to through non-search media. Consequently, assuming their ads are well written and targeted, these brands pay lower per-click costs in general, seemingly exploding the myth that the Internet is the great equalizer where no one knew whether or not a business was being run out of a garage. Although the brand discount may not seem fair, especially since much of the trumpeted claims about the PPC search marketplace is that it democratizes the marketplace, one can argue that there's nothing wrong with brand marketers paying lower prices than unknown marketers. After all, these brand marketers are simply leveraging the millions—perhaps billions—of dollars spent on advertising in the past, and as a result, consumers do in fact prefer and trust those brands. But the real problem is many new marketers are unaware of the degree to which the dice are loaded against them, and this is why so many find it difficult—if not impossible—to conduct search campaigns that meet their primary business objectives, whether they are to realize immediate ROI or to build market share.

4.3 Do Search Engines Have a Bias Against Segmentation?

We all know that the media landscape is fragmenting into ever smaller pieces, markedly reducing the value of the easily designed, mass-targeted advertising campaigns and making it imperative for all marketers to evolve their strategy and tactics. Segmentation, which involves identifying smaller groups of people and targeting them precisely, is a long-established technique in the direct-response segment of the advertising industry, and technology has allowed marketers to do a much better job of identifying likely in-market segments and then tailoring customized or personalized messages that are more likely to be perceived as relevant.

Google, Yahoo, and Microsoft's adCenter represent the most advanced incarnation of segmentation technology available today. In a keyword-based ad-serving environment, every keyword (and keyword combination) is tantamount to a separate channel, and search marketers are provided with an easy way to associate this unique channel with a custom-tailored creative message most likely to result in a click and (hopefully) a conversion. By carefully analyzing the keywords used, marketers can make inferences about where a given customer is in the "buy funnel." For example, a searcher entering the keyword "digital camera" is one most likely to be at the very earliest stage of this funnel, whereas one typing in "Nikon digital camera" is more likely to be part of the way through it. A searcher typing in "Nikon D50 SLR with 70–200mm lens" along with "free shipping" may be only a click away from consummating an online transaction.

The ability to infer intent from keyword combinations is one of the most powerful ways to identify and segment people and to then create custom-tailored messages aimed at urging the buying process forward. Additionally, today's search engines have deployed segmentation technologies that now include geographical and time-of-day (daypart) factors and are also in the process of introducing demographic and behavioral targeting that provide a much richer set of data from which marketers can draw conclusions about potential customers. When various segments are combined, accuracy is considerably enhanced, thus giving marketers unprecedented power to tailor advertising campaigns with unparalleled precision.

However, because this marketplace is designed to provide the marketplace proprietor (the search engine) with the maximum possible yield in clicks delivered at the highest price the market will bear, the hybrid-auction marketplace has an in-built tendency to discourage targeting. Although marketers selecting "long tail" keyword combinations in order to attract searchers who are more likely to be in-market will certainly pay less than they would for query terms more likely to be searched upon, they will also pay a penalty, given that the CTR/Adrank overlay rewards marketers with higher CTRs. In AdWords' early years, keywords that do not meet sufficient keyword activity thresholds were simply turned off because they were not judged to be profitable for Google to run. In 2005, however, Google modified its system to allow marketers to activate seldom clicked-upon keywords, but only if the marketer paid a minimum bid, which ranged widely for any given keyword. How exactly these minimum bids were calculated is unknown. (Google does not disclose any details of how it arrives at its activation thresholds to marketers, nor does it disclose many other details of how its ad server works, which has led marketers to consider its operation to be a black box.) But the practical effect of these minimums is that it is more costly for marketers to run targeted campaigns.

Google also does not allow marketers to see important details about the traffic against which clicks are bought on its search network. For example, it is impossible for marketers to distinguish clicks that came in through Google's main domain (google.com) from clicks from another portal for which Google provides search functionality, such as AOL. The AOL audience has unique properties, and so do those of the other portals and engines through which Google provides results, and some marketers would greatly benefit from being able to target campaigns directly at these users, while others might want to *not* have this audience exposed to their campaigns. But Google does not allow marketers to target their campaigns at this level, and enough marketers are clearly unhappy enough with this to wonder whether the motivation behind this decision is nothing more than the simple desire to maximize its own revenue-generating potential at the expense of marketers.

There are, however, third-party tools offered by third-party SEM agencies that can make it possible for marketers to separate the undifferentiated search traffic flowing through the search engines. These can provide real advantages for marketers and should be used whenever possible to identify the most desirable traffic to run ads against. Some third-party firms also provide basic campaign management systems that, although not as powerful as some of the in-house systems used at SEM agencies, are better than nothing.

4.4 Warning: the Search Marketplace Is Not a Mall

To some, the marketplace that Google and the other engines have created is akin to a vast shopping mall. Marketers advertise their wares on SERPs (Search Engine Results Pages), and users are driven to the individual stores within the mall to learn, shop, and buy.

But real malls don't work this way. They charge each store-owner a fixed rent each month, plus many also charge a percentage of sales. As long as retailers can exceed all their fixed costs, which include rent, salaries, and other fixed overhead, in addition to covering the variable costs included in their rent, they will be successful.

But what if the mall owner, after carefully looking at the amount of money he was taking in every year, devised a new business model specifically designed to maximize his profits? Rather than levying a fixed charge on each store owner, he instead instituted a system in which store owners would have to bid for space against each other. If each store owner began bidding for their space, how high would the bidding go? There's nothing preventing this bidding war from going up to the point where the profits of each store owner go to zero, forcing them to the level of near-zero profit, perhaps putting them completely out of business. The only way for these store owners to stay in business would be to:

1. have an amazing price advantage;
2. have a store much better merchandised at which shoppers buy much more frequently and at higher prices;
3. have some form of collusion—for example have all of the store

owners agree among themselves to not bid beyond a certain price for a given foot of space.

Ultimately, unless there were some strong anchor tenants with great buying power and merchandising, as its individual store owners spent all their profits in exchange for visibility, went out of business, and left it a "ghost mall," the mall owner that instituted such a bidding system for space would go out of business. That the search engines have not yet reached this point is because big retail brands and other strong Internet marketing players get the click-through-rate advantage of their brands, have buying power that maintains margins, and have sufficient scale to test and optimize their online stores for maximum conversion and high ticket cost.

4.5 A Search Engine Tax?

The cost of advertising and marketing has always been built into the price paid by the consumer for a given product. That a higher price may dissuade people from buying this product is ordinarily offset by advertising and marketing that can generate additional demand for this same product. By definition, in fact, a "brand" is that product or service that consumers are willing to pay more for because familiarity has engendered a sense of demand for that product. Search engines, however, do not create demand in the same way that print, radio, or television ads do. Instead, they work much like a Yellow Pages–style directory, where a preexisting demand is already in the user's mind. Even when a consumer is still researching a problem and will arrive at a commercial solution, the search engines in themselves are not a primary factor in moving the consumer down the path to purchase. Rather, the sites in the search results (which include reviews, ratings, advice, and educational information on every conceivable topic) shoulder the majority of the responsibility in helping consumers decide what to buy. More often than not, these sites stimulate more curiosity, which manifests itself in yet another search. Search engines perform a useful, necessary function by serving as a filter and aggregator, and they deserve to be paid for this service. But essentially this service is the collection a toll between the user searching for a given product or service and the business providing it. The marketer, not the searcher, pays the toll, which is factored into the calculation made to determine what the product or service can be sold for. Even brand names and domain names are bid on by their owners, their channel, and their competition.

There's absolutely nothing wrong with marketers paying to gain traffic (and hopefully, qualified leads and potential purchasers) to a search engine that delivers such people, and then passing the cost back to the consumer. But let's take a look at some additional accruing charges that are byproducts of the way this hybrid auction model works.

Let's take as our example a large online bank that is running paid search campaigns to direct users to its web site that promotes its services. The bank company buys keywords associated with its service and bids aggressively to secure top placement for its listings. This is done not only because it wants to be associated with a particular service offering but also because when customers are acquired in this way there is significant profit from the direct customer acquisition.

An existing customer who has a question about his statement or a problem with service types the brand name or the generic term they used to sign up originally into a search engine, sees the top-ranking ad, and without scanning below, where there actually is an organic listing reading "ACME Bank," clicks on the paid ad. The result is that the bank is charged several dollars. The user, now on the bank's landing page (which was designed to display an attractive offer to a buyer, not an existing customer with a question about his statement), hunts around for the "Contact Us" page, and finally finds what he was looking for: a toll-free 800 number. Picking up the phone, he calls the 800 number. The marketer now has paid two charges: first for the erroneous click and now for the 800 call. For marketers receiving thousands of queries per day, these costs can become significant.

What we're talking about here isn't click fraud (after all, the user didn't click on the wrong link intentionally or with any malice toward the company). Nor is there anything that the search engine necessarily can do about it: search engines may be smart but they're not telepathic and are not likely to be able to tell the difference between User A, who's actually interested in a setting up a new account to get a great rate on a money market account, and User B, who just wants to discuss a statement. Such inefficiencies are built into the search marketplace and they're not immediately obvious to marketers until they begin calculating the amount of money they've paid each month to the search engine and the amount of new sales they've experienced, and then tallied up a cost per order. At this point, they may scratch their heads and wonder why there's someone in the middle—the search engine collecting the toll—who's profited quite nicely from the confusion.

One might think the marketer should cancel their bidding and assume the consumer will find their site anyway. That may be true for the existing customer, but prospective customers are clicking through on that paid link as well. To turn off the paid listing would be the equivalent of marketing suicide. Even for brand terms it nearly always makes sense to bid. Doubling the screen real estate in the SERP and having the ability to fully control the user experience (title, description, and landing page) for the paid ad often increases the conversion rate on paid clicks over that of the organic (unpaid clicks).

The success of PPC search-engine marketing has essentially put marketers between a rock and a hard place. The "rock" is that to withdraw from having a presence in this marketplace is a perilous risk because it is likely their competitors have already established their positions and are chipping away at our marketerers' market share each day they are not present in the market. The "hard place" is that the inherent inefficiencies, such as the one alluded to above, are inescapable features of this marketplace whose only solution would come from a major change in the way search engines operate.

Can marketers do anything to fight these in-built market biases on their own? Yes, but, because hybrid auctions favor marketers whose ads are clicked on most frequently with significant discounts, it will cost them dearly. If an ad that would direct users to the service area of the cell phone company's site could be cheaply placed, this would provide a theoretical solution. But because a special ad reading something like "Click this ad for service only" would get a significantly fewer number of clicks, and because of the unique rules of the hybrid auction, such an ad would be prohibitively expensive to maintain. Additionally, the marketer is primarily interested in customer acquisition not customer maintenance; the marketer is focused on the searchers who are in-market and prospective customers.

Another option, again using the example above, would be that a user typing in the name of the bank and clicking on the paid listing could be presented with an intermediary page that might ask the user something else about their query. Were they interested in seeing their statement? If so, the user would be delivered to the bank's site without charging the bank. If, however, they were interested in opening an account, the search engine could pocket the money, and the marketer would happily pay this premium to have the chance to acquire a new customer. Unfortunately, the chances of something like this occurring are remote. Search engines have no necessary incentive to perform any kind of post-click qualifications simply because doing so would reduce their revenues. Their whole rationale has consistently been to squeeze the best possible monetization rates from their ad platforms. Unfortunately, many marketers find it impossible to live by these strange new rules, all of which seem to be to the advantage of the intermediary and toll-taking search engine.

However, being charged significant media and advertising dollars in order to talk to existing customers isn't unique to search. Much of what the advertising consumers see is in fact for products or services they already buy. Coke and Pepsi spend hundreds of millions of dollars promoting products nearly everyone knows quite well. The same is true for the automotive, banking, consumer products, travel, and retail sectors.

Ironically, for traditional offline advertising, the better targeted the media against the target audience, the greater the number of existing customers who will see the ad. This is because a marketer's best next customer probably shares a significant amount in common with the current customer. The key for the CMO is not elimination of duplicative advertising, but rather maximizing the impact of the advertising that touches those consumers who either have not made a decision in favor of the CMO's brand or are open to switching from the competition. Search-engine marketing reaches both the existing customer—thus reinforcing the brand—and the prospective customer. A well-crafted campaign influences both consumers positively.

4.6 The Click Fraud Conundrum

When outsiders discuss the PPC search marketplace, click fraud is often the first issue mentioned, and there's no doubt it's an issue that, unless redressed quickly, may become serious enough to endanger the future of the entire search-marketing industry. Google and the other engines have acknowledged the problem exists, and Google has notably already allocated $93 million in click credits in order to settle a class-action suit brought by marketers claiming massive click fraud.

How large is the click fraud problem? It depends on who you ask. Some analysts claim that the percentage of "invalid clicks" ranges as high as 30 percent. Others estimate it's much lower, somewhere around 10 percent. That's a big spread. Click fraud is a nettlesome issue not only because it clearly presents a cost of doing business that marketers should not have to pay for, but also because it belies the idea that everything that happens on the Internet—the most inherently measurable medium yet conceived—can be measured. And yet, on the other hand, there is something deeply disingenuous when the advertising establishment uses click fraud to attack the search marketplace. After all, the entire premise of valuing advertising via Nielsen or any other sample-based, estimation-reliant methods are laughably imprecise, especially when compared to the kind of granular quantification of consumer behavior that can be accomplished on the Internet. And it is equally clear that print publishers have played fast and loose with circulation numbers for some time, making their tirades against Internet-based advertising ring hollow.

Analysts, the press, and those in the business of monitoring for click fraud also neglect to mention that all the major search engines have systems in place to capture many of the invalid clicks caused by click fraud, robots, or even consumers engaging in repetitive search behavior. Once these invalid clicks have been removed from the equation, the click fraud problem looks much smaller.

Yet click fraud presents another trap into which marketers can and do fall regardless of whether the click fraud is authentic or has already been reconciled by the engines. Click fraud becomes an issue because of an intrinsic problem with how the CPC marketplace is set up. For example, Google's whole model is based on selling clicks to advertisers. Whether a click emanates from a real person seeking information from a marketer who has bought a given keyword, person with no intention of taking an action sought by the marketer, or even an automated robot (if that robot was not detected by Google's screening system), the search engine still gets paid. To use a very simple analogy, Google, at least from an economic perspective, would initially seem to be in exactly the same position as a bank would that had a liberal insurance policy guaranteeing it would be completely compensated for every dollar stolen without a rise in its premium. As long as the insurance company is willing to pay whatever the bank loses because of robbery, there is no immediate economic incentive for it to secure its assets. However, like a bank whose insurance rates *would* rise, Google's revenues from advertising would fall if it didn't police click fraud. Most larger marketers measure the post-click behavior of clicks from every engine and keyword. When invalid or fraudulent clicks are billed by the engines, the rational marketers in the marketplace drop their bids in order to maintain ROI on their campaigns. And an ad marketplace must maintain not only the loyalty of their advertisers, but their trust as well. The same is true for all the securities, currency, and commodities markets. The reason some countries' stock markets are preferred over others is directly related to the trust of the investor. When that trust is misplaced, the entire marketplace suffers.

The crux of the click fraud issue is that marketers shouldn't have to pay for clicks that aren't authentic or valid. A tangential issue to this is click quality. Not all clicks are equal in quality, And some clicks may not be suitable as media and, therefore, shouldn't be paid for, or are worth less than premium clicks. The goal here is to define and determine what makes a click billable. Even if we can achieve a black-and-white definition of a valid click, we 'are still left with the challenge of measuring the value or quality of those qualifying valid clicks.

Toward that end, several major Internet advertising players are attempting to tackle these very issues. The Search Engine Marketing Professional Organization (SEMPO), on whose board I have sat since its founding, is researching the issue of click quality; and the Interactive

Advertising Bureau (IAB), which championed and authored the industry standards for counting ad impressions, also launched an initiative to "create a set of Click Measurement Guidelines." Loss of marketer and advertiser confidence in the validity of clicks as well as concerns regarding the scope of the click fraud problem were major catalysts in moving this project forward. The IAB committees, including the Search Engine Committee, have for some time been discussing the need for clarity in click auditing, reconciliation, measurement, and definitions.

No doubt Google, Yahoo, Microsoft, Ask, and the other search engines have learned more about both advertiser perception of the click fraud issue and the confusion in the marketplace brought about by lawsuits as well as an explosion of companies offering only click fraud monitoring solutions. All the major engines support the IAB Click Measurement Working Group, as do the third-party ad-serving, click-counting, and campaign management companies. Just as impression fraud and the fuzzy way impressions were sometimes counted nearly derailed the online advertising business in its first decade, click-quality and -measurement standards are required in order to ensure all parties engaged in SEM are on the same page (pun intended).

Google even went so far as to start showing advertisers the valid and invalid clicks in AdWords reporting. It released a white paper (more of a research report) criticizing many players in the click fraud monitoring business as well as click fraud consultants for making fundamental analysis errors resulting in an overstatement of the click fraud problem. The report even named companies whose estimates Google claims are flawed.

Interestingly, some of the report's points will be the same issues that third-party research will have to reconcile when reviewing participant data. The biggest issues are undifferentiated visits and use of log files as a data source when counting inbound clicks. We have found inbound ad click redirects are the most accurate method for counting clicks and determining their source and frequency. Although Google isn't planning to issue credits to advertisers based on analysis it considers flawed, it has been the most active thus far in providing insight for marketers into the click fraud issue.

Perhaps we can start a dialogue on what exactly a billable click is. Let's start by listing those elements all parties can likely agree define an advertising click:

- A click is generated by a human, not a robot or automated spider.
- When a human creates a click, he/she does so consciously and with purpose.
- Humans who click are interested in navigating to a specific page or site.
- Humans understand clicking is a navigational action resulting in the browser loading the new page or site.

More nebulous areas relate to when a human-generated click with all the above intentions perhaps shouldn't be billable. Should a click be billable if:

- The person repeats the navigational behavior on the same exact page (SERP), resulting in a second click within a session or short period?
- The person clicks a link to the same advertiser on a different SERP (new keyword search) or from a different contextual or behavioral ad impression?
- The person is a competitor to the advertiser whose link is clicked?

If any of the above or other conditions invalidate a click, does the publisher, network, third party, or advertiser have the responsibility to reconcile the billable and invalid clicks? My guess is much of the work done by the IAB in defining and standardizing impressions will be valuable guides for how the standards will be set in the future.

Google and the other engines do have real incentives for doing something about click fraud, given that this problem, if left to fester, will lower bids, erode trust, and eventually drive advertisers away. But these incentives are softer and more remote from having a marketplace whose rules function in order to remove the economic incentive for fraud to occur. Unfortunately, the PPC marketplace has no such inbuilt set of disincentives, other than expulsion or lawsuits, for the publishers who cheat, which means that click fraud can be minimized but not completely eliminated. Some people postulate that a solution is to move to a model in which marketers will not pay the search engine or any other intermediaries for anything less than an actual conversion to a lead or sale. Such a performance-based model does exist in many discrete areas of the Internet economy, notably within affiliate networks, as well as in a handful of search engines—the most notable being Snap.com, a site whose advertising model is predicated on a business model wholly reliant upon delivering paying customers to marketers.

It is, however, too early to see whether a pay-for-performance model will be successful, and this is for a very simple reason: publishers, upon whose networks a sizeable percentage of PPC advertising runs, are exposed to more risk by running pay-for-performance ads than PPC ads. Until such a time when a system might be devised to equalize the comparative risk to publishers, pay-for-performance advertising will remain a tiny, relatively insignificant fragment of the overall interactive advertising industry. The vast majority of transactions will continue to occur through the established PPC-based engines: Google, Yahoo, Microsoft, and a handful of others.

There are many reasons that pay-for-performance is unlikely to replace the PPC marketplaces at the search engines:

- The cookies used to measure performance are often deleted by consumers or blocked by corporate firewalls.
- Performance-based models have difficulty recognizing the true value of the delivered site visitor.
- There is a branding impact to both the search listings and the resulting visits to marketer sites even if the purchase is not immediate.
- The majority of purchases are made offline even if online research played a key role in the purchase decision.
- Consumers switch computers during the purchase funnel (work/home).
- There is a channel relationship and the original equipment manufacturer (OEM) is doing the advertising.

In a marketplace that simultaneously supports CPA, CPC, and CPM advertising, with the exception of aggregators that sell leads on a nonexclusive basis to many marketers at the same time, the CPA advertising will generally mop up the leftovers. We see that situation in several vertical markets including the online education market as well as the online lending/mortgage market.

4.7 The SEO Trap

Given both the complexities of managing paid search campaigns and the costs, tangible and intangible, associated with them, marketers often are tempted to rely solely on "natural" (a.k.a. "organic" search results), both because they are "free" and because they seem at first glance to be relatively easy to obtain.

Although it is true that marketers do not have to pay the search engines to display organic results, this does not make the acquisition of such results "free." There are costs associated with achieving top organic rankings, either in expenditures associated with in-house marketing or IT staff who perform these services, or in services provided by an external search engine optimization team.

Given the high level of maintenance associated with running paid search campaigns, as well as the relatively low maintenance associated with SEO, it's tempting for marketers to believe they can rely on only organic rankings to provide the sufficient level of qualified traffic to make their digital marketing efforts successful. (Note: Although there are instances when web sites need to have considerable work done on them—for example, a site with hundreds of thousands of pages that are modified frequently—and there are cases in which sites need ongoing SEO services, many marketers can achieve most of the important optimization benefits without having to pay for ongoing consultancy services from an optimization firm.)

SEO is a vital task that needs to be accomplished. In fact, in order to ensure the destination site is fully vetted for all incoming traffic, whether generated by paid placements, organic SEO, or other means such as e-mail, viral marketing, etc., optimization should be performed well in advance of embarking on a paid search campaign. The mistake to be avoided, however, is to believe that high organic rankings obviate the need for paid search campaigns. Some of our own clients have wondered what would happen if, once they had achieved their SEO objectives (number one organic rankings on the keywords that drive most of their traffic), they simply shut down their paid campaigns and pocketed the money they had been spending on those keywords.

We have actually run such tests at the request of these clients, and conversions declined 48 and 65 percent. This happened regardless of the excellent SEO and top rankings enjoyed by these clients, or even that their branded keywords converted measurably better than unbranded ones. Sometimes it only takes a few hours for a client to see the mistake made, at which point the client contact calls and asks to reactivate the campaign. The dramatic loss in conversions for those clients with high organic keyword position who choose to shut down paid campaigns can be traced to several sources, such as:

1. competitive saturation causes loss in clicks to competitors;
2. loss of clicks to their own channel (affiliates or other licensees); and
3. higher conversion rates on the PPC landing pages than the pages selected by the search engines as most relevant.

Fluctuating and escalating keyword prices, increasing competition, unpredictable changes to the search engines' algorithms, and unquantifiable evils such as click fraud are enough to strike fear into the heart of even the hardiest marketers. For these reasons, it's no wonder so many persist in believing that a paid search strategy is optional and that SEO alone will do the job. This idea, while comforting, is a dangerous illusion. To succeed, marketers need to use every weapon in their arsenal, and to evaluate each methodology not only in terms of cost, but also ROI, market share growth, and instrumentality in achieving strategic business objectives. Advertising and PR coexist, as should paid and organic search marketing.

4.8 Solutions: Adjust to the New Unknowables

Although the marketing systems created by the search engines promise to deliver accountability and transparency, there are many pitfalls. How do you avoid them?

The first decision you'll need to make before you embark into this new, promising, but perilous digital marketing environment is one of allocation of tasks, roles, and responsibilities. Should you attempt to build an internal team capable of handling these tasks, or should you outsource them to an external agency? There is no right or wrong answer to this question. In-house teams, equipped with a requisite level of automation, staffed with smart people, and given enough latitude by management to seek out and exploit fast-rising opportunities can be competitive with external agencies, especially those that do not devote equal resources to a specific digital marketing campaign. Additionally, not all outsourced options are equal when it comes to managing auction-media campaigns including PPC search.

Like it or not, digital marketing is not and never will be a completely accountable and programmable marketing discipline. People—smart and well-trained—need to be in the loop in order to analyze, interpret, and, if necessary, override the operation of any automated system because there will always be "unknowns" that one has never anticipated. Also, the digital marketing environment is inherently unstable. Even if you know a lot about what works and doesn't work in your own digital marketing campaign, you will always know much less about the strategies and tactics used by competitors. Those running the marketplace—although today they're the search engines, tomorrow they might be someone else—will probably never let marketers enjoy a transparent view into how they run their markets. Some ambiguity will always be with us; some level of waste, unaccountability, and perhaps even fraud will also always exist in the process. These evils have all persisted in analog marketing for many years, but have been cloaked by the completely unaccountable nature of analog media. By investing in the most powerful resources, the best teams, and the best automated systems, you will be able to minimize these evils, but you will never be completely free of them. That's just the way the digital marketing cookie crumbles.

CHAPTER 5

20:20 Vision
Branding Is Not Dead

"There has been no corporate mandate to cut ad spending as a percent of sales, only to spend all marketing money more efficiently,"

—P&G CMO Jim Stengel, quoted in *Advertising Age*, 12/15/06

*

BRAND MARKETERS have always been cautious about the degree to which their traditional branding objectives, accomplished in expensive and immersive thirty- or sixty-second-spot commercials broadcast to immense audiences, can be translated to digital media. In a fragmented media world, the process of branding is less about touching heartstrings than providing opportunities to engage the consumer more deeply with a brand's unique promise. This means understanding media interaction effects between online and offline media, and then designing metrics that can serve as proxies for customers' engagement with a given brand online. If marketers are going to influence consumers' buying behavior positively, they must remain relevant to each of their consumers.

Because many early adopters of digital marketing came from a background of direct marketing rather than "mainstream" advertising, the conclusion that branding potential was minimal in this environment could be expected. But the relevant question now concerns how branding is being redefined by the advent of digital media and search marketing.

5.1 How Digital Marketing Redefines the Branding Process

Because consumers have so profoundly changed their media consumption behavior, brand marketers must approach online media accordingly. Today, people consume media asynchronously and simultaneously. It's not unusual for people to have several media devices in use at once: watching TV while chatting online (or via SMS on cell phones), using search engines, and navigating to destination web sites. In fact, often search engine use is stimulated by the content being consumed in other media, particularly TV.

When the Media Center at the American Press Institute and a firm called BigSearch jointly surveyed this phenomenon in late 2003, it found that 70 percent of media consumers used multiple media simultaneously. The Mobium Creative Group discovered an even more astounding finding in 2004: 80 percent of businesspeople use more than one medium at once. One important consequence of simultaneous media consumption is that traditional brand marketing methods aimed at demanding undivided attention are not effective in a multichannel environment. But those marketers who are able to think of branding in a way that works across a variety of media, both analog and digital, can reap rewards that extend and deepen their target audience's involvement in their brands in a way that was never possible in noninteractive media.

Many brand advertisers have discovered that digital marketing provides an effective adjunct, if not an actual substitute, to traditional untargeted advertising, and this new behavior is reflected in advertising spending trends. As the chart below shows, many brands are

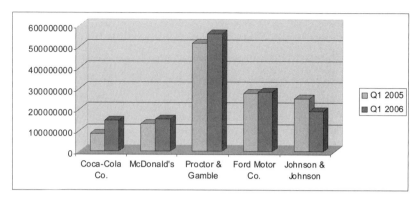

Top Five Brands: TV Advertising: Q1 2005–Q1 2006.
Source: TNS Media Intelligence, reprinted in *Promo* Magazine, August 2006.

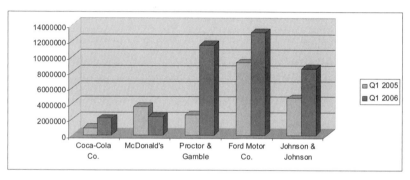

Top Five Brands: Internet Advertising: Q1 2005-Q1 2006. Source: TNS Media
Intelligence, reprinted in *Promo* Magazine, August 2006

increasing investment in online media while they are also moderating
their investment in television.

Branding through traditional channels, including broadcast TV,
print, outdoor, PR, and via event marketing, is not going to disappear,
but it will be redefined. The world does not begin and end with the
thirty-second spot, nor with any single channel or platform, whether it
be digital or analog. Instead, exposure to any branded experience,
online or off, initiates a chain of user interactions that extend into

cyberspace and often rebound back into the offline world. And after being stimulated to the level of curiosity by offline media, the first touch point the user tends to select is the search engine or direct navigation to the brand's web site. Being visible in the search results is critical, and it is amazing that many marketers do not understand that, unless they have established a presence, the user is likely to move in a different direction—whether that means losing interest or being drawn to the site of a competitor. Assuming the consumer has engaged in a successful search or navigated directly to the brand's web site, the second touch point is then at the destination web site, which is the central hub of the online branding experience: the place where a user can engage and be immersed in the brand marketer's chosen self-image.

With brand web sites, the marketers must cater to the diverse needs and desires of their market while simultaneously reinforcing the brand. For e-commerce sites, this means the site must not only be a great online store, But it also must provide easy access to account and prior order information, FAQs, ratings, reviews, and possibly even the consumer's ability to interact with the site as content creators.

5.2 Why Brand Marketers Are Confused

Brand marketers interested in pursuing digital marketing need to acquaint themselves with the diverse methods of planning for digital marketing campaigns. The traditional media purchasing model involves reaching a limited set of objectives, including impressions, reach, frequency, target audience, and gross rating points (GRPs). However, in a digital era when consumers of advertising travel fragmented channels and whose characteristics can be more succinctly identified, brand marketers need to evolve their thinking about *how* to reach out and engage these consumers in a way that is more relevant, less intrusive, and more effective.

To be effective in a fragmented media landscape, much of which is digital, the brand message can no longer be the same across all media and across all audience segments. When consumer's have the ability to control what they see—or at least when and how to pay attention to media, the means of enticing them to absorb and interact with the brand's message must be more relevant than ever before. Even the humor that can be used effectively to break through TV clutter must be combined with a relevant brand message in order to achieve branding objectives.

Additionally, unlike the thirty-second spot, search-engine marketing provides limited opportunities to generate the feelings that invoke engagement and connection to a brand image in a plain-Jane text ad. With only twenty-five characters followed by two lines of thirty-five characters each, brand marketers are unable to tell a story. The advantage, however, is that the search ad itself isn't a complete ad message: it's only the beginning of the ad experience, whether or not the ad is immediately clicked. When the ad is clicked, the engagement then continues at the marketer's site, where the rich media experience can be enjoyed and the marketer can make full use of the increasingly TV-like properties permitted on a site accessed over a broadband network. However, because in this advertising environment the consumer is in control and requires the ability to navigate a path according to his specific needs, marketers must think nonlinearly about their company's web sites.

This holistic view carries the idea of media beyond simply ad delivery to ad and branding message consumption, because it is this consumption over time that generates emotional responses. When prior messages are restimulated in a certain environment correlated with the purchase event, this sustained media consumption establishes emotional triggers that cause consumers to favor one particular brand.

Recently, there has been a lot of buzz around engagement as being a new metric of advertising and media success. Often the discussion includes a concept called "co-creation," in which the consumer partici-pates in the creation of what the brand means to him. Effective brand-ing strategies today must involve the customer in an active journey of discovery through a thousand digital nooks and crannies, and search is typically among the first entry points a user passes when beginning this journey.

Brand marketers, especially of consumer packaged goods (CPGs) consumed by wide swaths of the general populace, will always seek to develop media strategies that deliver ad messages across the widest reach, using the greatest tonnage, and delivering the largest scale. Waste remains a secondary consideration. But because advertising that is more relevant is better suited to cutting through the media clutter, even CPG marketers can benefit from utilizing better targeting.

5.3 Why Brands Have an Advantage Online

Search marketing should always be part of a larger marketing strat-egy. Although it should not be the only medium, any holistic inte-grated marketing strategy is amplified when search is included. The primary lessons of Media and Marketing 101 apply also in the digital world: to reach your objectives, always buy the most efficient media first. If advertising in search engines outperforms other media, you're overspending on other media and underspending on search. The rule is to allocate each media dollar where it works hardest. Unfortunately, although this is a great rule of thumb that holds true most of the time, reality is more complex, and search impressions, clicks, and, in par-ticular, the perceived relevance of a particular ad to a searcher are driven by offline PR, media, and advertising messages. Thus, there is a strong interaction effect among media, particularly search and other media. Most marketers don't have access to media allocation models that can account for these interactions or multiplier effects, and many don't even understand how to approach measuring these interaction effects. At even the most sophisticated traditional ad agencies, media mix modeling currently under way still fails to include online and search.

Off- and online media purchases clearly drive not only brand awareness but even search behavior on core keywords. For example, "American Idol" is a top-ten search term week after week during the season (along with the contestants' names). The acronym "NASCAR" and its participating drivers also are heavily searched. When golf matches are feted on magazine covers and sports shows, Tiger Woods and other celebrity spokespersons are top search terms. Look no further than Carl's Jr. Hamburgers and Paris Hilton to see the role search plays in any integrated marketing plan.

Marketers advertising heavily on TV and other broadcast media consistently see the following effects exerted from users who are either simultaneously or sequentially accessing Internet search engines:

- Search volume on brand and product names goes up. Consumers see the brand, get curious, and often search for the brand or product name rather than follow the ad's instructions to visit the URL directly. Some surfers seem to think all navigation should be through search, and clearly Yahoo, Google, and Microsoft won't dissuade that practice. That means search volume on the URL or the brand (which is generally similar or the same as the center section of the full URL) spikes dramatically.

- Search volume on the issues discussed in the ad also goes up, though this effect is harder to measure. When products are advertised to solve a problem (e.g., heartburn, loneliness, job search, erectile dysfunction, vacations, commercial-free radio), the incremental search volume on the issues themselves may be even higher than the domain. Essentially, the ad creates interest in the category from which all advertisers and others in the search results benefit.

- Click-Through Rates on the advertiser's existing ads go up. The CTR increase is measurable for both branded keywords as well as generic, nonbranded keywords. This is particularly true if the ad budget is significant and the ad is successfully creating recall and awareness.

5.4 Quantifying the Brand Advantage

Search marketing, because the playing field is intrinsically tilted toward brands, is an attractive medium for brand-oriented advertisers to explore. As searchers prefer to click on ads that are familiar, relevant, and compelling, hybrid-auction systems give brands a huge discount on top positions, thereby raising the Click Through Rate, and allowing these advertisers achieve higher visibility—all the while paying less for it. Although discount has existed for years within Google's advertising system, with the advent of a Quality Score overlay rewarding marketers whose ads are clicked on more frequently, it has become even more pronounced. Quality Score takes into account factors beyond historical Click-Through Rates when calculating the predicted CTR for a particular ad in a specific situation. Additionally, regardless of position, the brand term in the ad copy or branded domain also seems to influence predicted CTR.

Major brands, as well as sellers of their products and services, can take advantage of this brand discount. However, if you don't sell brands and aren't a brand in your own right (in terms of having a domain most people would recognize and associate with your product or service), you can always hope your competition makes some tactical or strategic errors or writes ads that are so boring and generic that, regardless the brand effect, your ads are more exciting and compelling and can tip the scales in your favor.

When purchasing media or crafting marketing plans, brand advertisers traditionally think of target customers from a demographics perspective. For instance, Microsoft's adCenter allows marketers to "bid boost" by age and gender; brand marketers will respond to this because it is the first time search marketing discusses targeting in familiar terms. Over time, direct marketers will learn to love the bid boost, as they determine if certain age and gender combinations result in higher conversions, higher immediate profit, or higher lifetime customer value.

5.5 Brand Lift and Search Marketing

Marketers have been ever advancing to paid search marketing because they are increasingly seeking to put their products and services in front of users who are actively pursuing information in their product/service category. This trend was illustrated in the two most recent (2005 and 2006) Search Engine Marketing Professionals Organization (SEMPO) state-of-the-market surveys, each canvassing the attitudes on search marketing of over 500 search engine advertisers and SEM agencies.

Many brand marketers, however, have expressed doubt about whether search-based advertising provided any meaningful brand lift. These marketers are more likely to perceive the benefits of online advertising in a form that more closely resembles the traditional thirty-second spot, namely so-called "rich media" advertising, targeted by demographics or psychographics, not keywords.

In a 2004 study conducted by the Search Committee of the Internet Advertising Bureau, this question was forever put to rest. The study, which used 10,500 randomly selected participants, showed pages representing SERPs and contextual articles running PSA ads to both a control group and to a group in which the brand had a more favorable position on the page. Test participants were shown brand ads appropriate to each page and asked questions whose aim was to determine brand attitudes and recall. In order to limit self-selection and exposure bias, respondents were not told in advance the subject of the study was advertising. The results were clear and unambiguous:

> On average, when respondents were asked to name a specific leading brand within a tested industry, they were 27 percent more likely to name the brand displayed in the top spot compared to a control group not exposed to the ad.

Unaided brand awareness jumped from 43.9 percent for the control group to 55.6 percent for the top position. (Most brand marketers consider unaided brand awareness scores a highly valid measurement of advertising effectiveness). However, this study did not take into account the even more compelling factor of post-click branding, which occurs after the click onto the advertiser's web site.

5.6 Branding Opportunities in Keywords

Some brand marketers are already involved with search, but those new to the medium should enter and buy listings in order to enhance their on- and offline branding campaigns. For some of the largest brands, inventory levels for most search words directly attributed to their brands are quite low. Even Coke and Pepsi only see monthly searches in the 100,000 range for their brands, and nearly none for generic terms such as "cola" and "thirst quencher." Even if Click-Through Rates reach 10 percent, search spending and the total impressions only represent a comparative drop in their marketing buckets.

One way to expand a campaign is to associate brands with the problems they solve or attributes they wish to portray ("grass stain," "sexy car," "healthy meal," "clear cellular," "fast meal," etc.). The upside of this strategy is that the brander increases unaided awareness at the precise time searchers are open to a message regarding a solution to their problem. The downside is that there is that there really isn't much inventory available for purchase.

However, brand marketers eager to capitalize on search listings' ability to increase brand awareness do have an alternative to limiting their selection to low-volume keywords. For instance, many major brands sponsor sports or entertainment events, And query volume on sports and entertainment keywords typically runs high. In some cases, the costs per click for keywords associated with sports, sports personalities, TV shows, movie characters, or actors are reasonable compared to average costs per click. If the brand has relevant content on its site (or can generate it inexpensively), the promotion sponsorship keywords (PSKs) are a powerful branding opportunity, particularly when coupled with the Branding Effectiveness Index (BEI). Brand marketers should look at PSKs the same way as promotions: the PSKs extend the promotion's or sponsorship's value and multiply the brand's visibility in relation to the original promotion, sports event, person, or entertainment.

Here are some examples of how marketers can use PSKs:

- Coke could buy "American Idol," the judges' names, and all the stars' names, as well as the NASCAR personalities' names. Coke spends a reported $25 million per season to associate itself with *American Idol*. It's natural for searchers to associate Coke with the show, and a site with relevant content would provide an unparalleled branding experience for those conducting searches on the show and its stars.
- If Coke didn't buy the clicks, perhaps Ford or Cingular (becoming once again AT&T) should take up the slack.

- Hewlett-Packard could buy *Shrek* terms, as well as Magic Johnson (HP works with his foundation).
- Buick or Accenture could buy "Tiger Woods" and other related golf terms.
- Callaway, PING, and Nike should all buy the names of the pro golfers who use their equipment, as well as the names of their caddies.
- McDonald's should buy "Neopets," "Tony Hawk," "LPGA," Olympic keywords, and World Cup terms.
- Nike should buy "Serena Williams," "Michael Jordan," and all Olympic-related terms, including major athletes' names.

When buying personalities as keywords, it's important to monitor the news, just in case external events could create negative brand associations (e.g., Martha Stewart for Kmart, Kobe Bryant for McDonald's, or Whoopi Goldberg for Slim-Fast). Although the opportunity for brand marketers to leverage the power of SEM through a variety of means, the campaigns must be monitored actively and vigilantly.

Brand marketers aren't the only ones bidding on their own brand keywords. Both the channel and the competition may also bid on brand names in Google (although the brand is not allowed to appear in the competing ad). Some product brands are heavily bid upon by retailers authorized to sell that brand's products. Pampers, iPod, ThinkPad, QuickBooks, and CoolPix are all sold by retailers with online presences. Corvette, F-150, and Chris-Craft are bid on by sales channels for those brands. Brand owners must decide if they want to bid on these keywords, regardless of whether they themselves have an online store.

The decision by the brand holder to bid when there is already an active channel and that brand does not sell direct is not a trivial one. Most retailers and other channel partners (in travel, insurance, and web hosting) are not exclusive to one brand. Therefore there is a real risk the retailer will capture a customer on one brand term and sell a competing brand. In that case, the brand has ceded control to "partners" but risks losing a customer permanently if a cross-sell to another brand occurs.

5.7 Solutions: Think Holistically, but Act Practically

Digital media do not exist in a vacuum. Media consumers are consuming media everywhere, and effective media planning means thinking less about individual media placements and more about fields of influence.

Search media is typically reactive: it responds to messages consumed elsewhere, and is therefore valuable as a barometer of the effectiveness of nonsearch marketing campaigns. Reaching consumers in an era of media fragmentation is not a matter of defining a single place to reach our fleeting consumer but rather analyzing how multiple media touch points work with each other and then tailoring messages that take maximal advantage of each media the consumer encounters.

Examples of this kind of holistic thinking are increasingly prevalent, as ad agencies have begun embedding messages in their broadcast TV spots instructing consumers to google their products. Additionally, large CPG companies have realized web sites can provide storytelling and branding possibilities not available through linear, one-way media such as television. Recently, Unilever's *Dove Evolution* video claimed more than 3 million online views and spurred thousands of accesses to Unilever's corporate sites. As a result of *Dove Evolution's* viral success, it was also featured on several mainstream TV programs, including *The View*, *Ellen*, *CNN*, *Entertainment Tonight*, and Fox's *Geraldo*. Essentially, *Dove Evolution* accomplished a positive feedback loop in which offline and online media worked together to maximize the best of both. Had it been confined to broadcast media, none of this would have happened. And there were no media carrying charges here, unlike Dove's SuperBowl spot, which cost it $2.5 million to run. (http://www.marketingvox.com/archives/2006/10/31/dove_evolu-tion_goes_viral_with_triple_the_traffic_of_super_bowl_spot/)

5.8 Solutions: Model Branding Interaction Effects

This stimulation of online search behavior from offline marketing efforts enables marketers to also use consumer search behavior as a means of measuring their overall marketing efforts, including their branding campaigns. In order to determine this, the appropriate analytics software needs to be installed, And doing so is a worthwhile investment: Web and campaign analytics are more than a reporting method—they are also a means to more effectively manage ad campaigns. Factors that help you measure your campaign success through experiential branding include:

- *Time on site.* The longer a visitor stays on the site after arriving via a search ad, the better job you've done as a marketer.
- *Page views.* The more pages the visitor interacts with, the greater the likelihood he or she has absorbed your marketing message. That's an increase in branding metrics (awareness, purchase intent, etc.).
- *Registrations.* The visitor gives your brand permission to engage in a dialogue. The ongoing conversation provides the opportunity to further build your brand and move the customer closer to purchase.
- *Download/view.* If your brand has a reputation for highly informative (e.g., movie or political ads) or highly entertaining (e.g., GEICO or Carl's Jr.) advertising, visitors may actually choose to play your video or audio advertising.

- *Configuration or comparison.* If your brand stacks up favorably against the competition and you provide a comparison page, that comparison can contribute significant value. Product configurators are also brand immersive (e.g., automotive, washing machines, computer, appliances, furniture).
- *Targeted link to retailers.* Many marketers don't directly sell products, but their sites support retailers through links. If search listings ultimately result in a link to a retailer, that's enhanced purchase intent. No branding metric is better than purchase intent.

By closing the data loop and adjusting a search campaign based upon site-side factors correlating with branding, marketers can take the mystery out of search marketing for branding. They can also allocate a branding budget more efficiently to whatever media channels they are currently using or intend to use.

5.9 Solutions: Use BEI and Site Engagement as Proxies for Measuring Branding Effectiveness

Beyond simple site-side behaviors, it's possible to measure the effectiveness of branding even more precisely, provided that a model is constructed in order to generate meaningful information on this effectiveness. As always, with better measurement comes better media management.

We propose a new metric, based on a behavior mapping strategy called the Branding Effectiveness Index, or BEI (pronounced "buy"). Although the BEI is a work in progress, it has already proven useful in comparing campaign results. The primary goal of the BEI is to quantify the branding impact resulting from a visitor's interaction with a web site, specifically observing visitors' actions that are an effect of a long-term brand metrics lift. The quantification of brand lift by behavior can either be measured through survey intercept or be assigned relative values by a marketer using values based on common sense.

Of course, each marketer's branding needs are unique, and each must determine which measurable actions and metrics to combine in order to create a unique BEI. The objective should always be to design a flexible metric that measures branding impact and the effectiveness of the site on a visitor who has already acted (clicked) on that ad unit, but not to measure the effectiveness of any given ad unit.

The following metrics can be used to build your own BEI.

- Purchase
- Registration
- Newsletter subscription
- Information request
- Page view
- Content depth or involvement
- Webinar view

To generate your own BEI, set the most valuable measurable action to a value of one. Other significant actions should be assigned a percentage value of that variable, based on importance. For example, if newsletter registration is your most valuable measurable action, and a brochure request is 70 percent as important as that, assign brochure request a value of 0.7. All actions are then added up and multiplied by their factor, and these are then totaled and divided by spending in order to determine the relative BEI for different media options.

Any campaign or campaign segment (even a single keyword listing) can be measured by how well it did in terms of achieving BEI. Using the example above, twenty newsletter registrations and ten newsletter requests for a $1,000 spend results in a BEI of $((20 \times 1)+(10 \times .7))/1,000$, or 0.027. If the number of newsletter registrations rises to forty for a different campaign segment, BEI is 0.047. This value is useful in comparing campaign segments when using the same formula. Of course, if a second campaign with a different set of measurable actions exists, then these results are not comparable.

A simpler way to think of BEI is as a variable, like a weighted average cost-per-action (CPA) that incorporates a host of post-click actions.

Let's look at *AdAge*'s top brands to see what metrics they might use to build BEI.

- *AT&T*. Although AT&T is a brand marketer, customers can purchase from it online. Therefore, the company might include a variety of other metrics in a BEI campaign index. If customer acquisition is the highest valued action (1), loyalty program signup might be 0.4 and interaction with a plans and services page might be 0.15.
- *Chevrolet*. Chevrolet has a brochure request, a dealer locator, a "Contact Us" form, content, and a clubs listing. All these measurable actions could be combined to form an overall BEI.
- *Ford*. Ford emphasizes newsworthy information, such as special financing rates. Perhaps that's its most important metric for building BEI, or perhaps it's a visit to "Build Your Ford."
- *Toyota*. Toyota is pushing the Camry. The company may use interaction with the brand's pages as a large BEI factor. If an event such as a page view is likely to repeat, it can be assigned a BEI factor relative to another, less frequent action. Different pages can also be assigned different factors. Sweepstakes entries might have a factor of 1, page views within the Camry section a factor of 0.03 per page view.
- *McDonald's*. McDonald's has a restaurant locator and may assign that the factor of 1, purchase of merchandise at 0.9, and visits to the "Treasure Planet Happy Meal" site area a 0.2.

5.10 Solutions: Practice Defensive Branding

Even if you don't use digital marketing to extend and deepen your brand experience online, you must always have a plan to defend your brand if and when you lose control of the conversation about it. For example, a recent outbreak of E-coli poisoning has been traced to several stores in the fast-food chain Taco Bell, and no one has found the cause. Understandably, Taco Bell sales are down, but the chain is more concerned that its brand name might be inextricably associated in the public's mind with the disease E-coli.

How did Taco Bell respond to this crisis? It instructed its PR agency to devise a campaign that would stress its proactive involvement in finding the culprit, and the agency launched a campaign called "Food Is Safe," with full-page ads being placed in the *New York Times*, *USA Today*, and others.

Unfortunately, neither Taco Bell nor its agency realized the crucial importance of online reputation management. As a result, users typing in the keywords "Taco Bell" were greeted not by a link to any properties associated with Taco Bell's "Food Is Safe" campaign, but rather saw ads from lawyers advertising E-coli lawsuits, an ad from a site called food-poisoning.com, and links to stories recounting the outbreak in the *Washington Post*. While there was (in the organic listing section of Google's SERPs), a link to Taco Bell's official home page, there was nothing on this site regarding the "Food Is Safe" PR campaign, or anything even acknowledging the public's concern about food safety at Taco Bell.

It's hard to understand why it didn't occur to Taco Bell's agency that anybody would be searching the keywords "Taco Bell" on the Web, especially when its brand name was being broadcast (in a very negative light) on radio and television news reports as well as in newspaper reports to millions of people each day. Understanding this is especially difficult when we know that Taco Bell's agency could have taken a few thousand dollars away from the thousands of dollars dumped into newspaper ads (which are not cheap) to buy its own branded key-words. But because some piece was missing from the equation, in cyberspace, this incident was a PR disaster.

There's a lot to learn from this PR misstep. You may be in control of your brand most of the time, but you have to plan for instances when you will lose control. When bad things happen and your brand is appropriated without your intention, you need to form a response that utilizes the interaction of both offline and online media behavior. Search engine behavior is largely reactive: people hear a news item or read an article, and then start hunting. When they arrive at a query point where your brand is, you have an opportunity to reach and inter-act with them. But if you aren't there, others (in this case class-action lawyers) will be all too ready to oblige.

Some brand marketers may believe they can coast along on high organic rankings, but this course can be risky, especially in cases where Effective Organic Position rates are depressed by other elements com-peting for scarce SERP real estate. Furthermore, relying on organic list-ings alone deprives the marketer of a powerful opportunity to establish a marketing touch point (perhaps with complementary messaging) that is tailored for searchers who have already demonstrated an under-standing of a given brand's equity. Conversely, as competing marketers learn how to tap the power of their competitors' brands when those brands generate searches may not be favorable to your client's trade-marks, it will become increasingly important for the brand holders to consider the possible negative impact of remaining passive in the paid search marketplace. I anticipate some changes in marketing budgets as brands realize they are giving huge gifts to their competition by staying out of paid search.

CHAPTER 6

Eye of the Robot
Technology Is Central (But It Isn't Enough)

"The first rule of any technology used in a business is that automation applied to an efficient operation will magnify the efficiency. The second is that automation applied to an inefficient operation will magnify the inefficiency."

—Microsoft Chairman Bill Gates

*

DESPITE THE CENTRALITY of technology in the digital media management process, perils arise for those who fail to see its intrinsic role in today's marketplace and integrate its operation with a cogent strategy for achieving one's business objectives.

The complexity of administering all but the simplest digital marketing campaigns requires the implementation of technology to manage these campaigns' multiple components. Sophisticated marketers typically deploy campaign management software capable of overseeing the multiple and ever-changing variables. In real-time media marketplaces, however, technology must control spending based upon what a given ad unit is worth in comparison to all the alternative options, and the permutations of possible media allocation outcomes are beyond the scope of traditional media buyers. Additionally, to fully leverage the larger segments of a market, mass-personalization may be required in order to keep the consumer's interest throughout the consumer-engagement process. Consequently, although technology is a necessary component in any successful digital marketer's arsenal, its operation must be supervised by skilled human operators capable of translating marketers' core objectives into effective and efficient marketing campaigns.

Digital marketing techniques have given increased levels of control to marketers, but the hidden cost of this control is complexity. Having access to technology appropriate for managing the complex technical environment required of digital marketing is a necessary—but insufficient—condition of success. Because digital marketing is not a set-and-forget process, but rather one that requires continual optimization through a feedback loop continually reporting meaningful intelligence that can be acted upon, a culture of testing is essential. Some think complexity and the need for technology and smart marketers will dissipate as the engines and ad marketplaces simplify their interfaces and add tools. Yet across the on- and offline advertising ecosystem, one thing is clear: consumers control the ads they pay attention to and those they choose to interact with. Consequently, targeting and relevance must always improve, but technology can only do so much of the work. Your site and business must be in synch with your marketing campaign and in tune with consumers' willingness to engage.

6.1 Basic Digital Marketing Issues

Marketing money is scarce, time is scarcer, and at the end of the day, you're judged by the results you achieve, not the technologies you've evaluated. For these reasons, many marketers have chosen search because it provides power, flexibility, and at least partial transparency. But it also comes with its own set of tough subchoices, ones that marketers need to make whether they're launching a new search campaign or tweaking one that has already been up and running. These include the following:

Which Search Engine?

Google, with nearly a 50 percent share of search queries, is naturally the preferred choice for many marketers because it delivers an enormous volume of clicks. With an immense distribution network that pushes ads through other well-trafficked portals such as AOL, Lycos, Ask.com, and others, you can reach more people with a Google campaign than with any other search engine.

But just because Google is number one doesn't mean that you should ignore the lower-trafficked engines such as Yahoo, Microsoft, and Ask.com. They might not be able to deliver the click-volume of Google, but they may offer you better conversion rates (our own studies of conversion rates bear this statement out). Depending on your business, you might also investigate IYPs (Internet Yellow Pages) or shopping comparison engines.

Running a multi-engine search campaign involves more work than running a campaign on just one engine, which is one reason many marketers prefer to either deploy technology that can automate this process or outsource the task to an agency.

Which Keywords?

The cornerstone of your campaign strategy is the keywords you select. But do you "go broad" to capture more traffic (at the risk of suffering a lower conversion rate and lower immediate ROI), or narrow-cast your selection to those keywords most likely to be used by your prospects when they're in the mood to buy something? Always remember that broad terms ("digital camera") may not provide any immediate ROI, but you may still need them because many users hunting for product information execute multiple searches, refining these queries as they grow closer to an action. Unless you've bought the broad terms that lead them into the buy funnel, it will be more difficult to catch their interest with a lower-volume, higher-converting specific phrase (such as "Nikon D50 with 200mm telephoto lens") that they'll see when they're closer to the end. (Note: whichever keywords you choose, you'll need to monitor their performance continually to separate performers from nonperformers. Make sure you've built your campaigns with enough granularity to do this. In Google, this means breaking out each keyword into its own Ad Group.)

Which Technology?

Google and the other engines have made it easy to get up and running with a basic PPC ad campaign in a matter of minutes. But as your campaign grows in size, you may discover that you need to make more changes—and more frequently—to your campaign in order to ensure its profitable operation. Because the price and position of PPC ads are assigned dynamically in a real-time auction, unless it's tweaked, a campaign that's profitable 1 p.m. may be failing by 4 p.m.

There are many off-the-shelf ROI-based campaign management tools that can help you replace those time-consuming manual campaign management tasks that can turn running PPC campaigns into an insufferable grind. Although they can provide relief for those struggling to run campaigns manually, it is impossible for any technology vendor to provide an "off-the-shelf" tool that can automatically make your campaigns profitable. And a good tool alone doesn't equal a maximally efficient or profitable as campaign. Tools, however valuable, will never be aware of the details of your business operations, your competitive landscape, or your business goals, but instead must be operated skillfully by those who are.

In-house or Outsourced?

Many small marketers I speak to are running their search campaigns in-house. This does involve costs, some of which are easily quantifiable (paying staff, licensing technology, and training) as well as some that are less tangible, such as opportunities missed (what other initiatives could these people have pursued had they not been charged with managing the campaign?). Unfortunately, in many organizations, the task of search is simply added to the workload of employees (typically in the marketing or IT departments) who already have full and critical responsibilities. Although it's possible that such overworked personnel can conduct a profitable campaign, it's also possible that they'll fail.

However, if you lack the internal resources to carry out effective search campaigns, outsourcing may make sense for your business. The best SEM agencies will conduct extensive consultations about your business goals, a highly customized campaign, frequent reporting, and a measurably higher ROI than what is possible with an in-house search campaign. Agencies usually work on percentage of media spend, and they justify these fees by (hopefully) demonstrating that such costs will always be less than the profits realized through a more efficient campaign.

6.2 Advanced Digital Marketing Issues

Managing digital media presents a problem much more complex than planning in the days of analog media. As we've seen from our discussion of search media, each keyword is essentially a channel that must be managed individually. But this channel is not a static thing: it can and should be programmed to yield maximum impact to each and every member of an ever-changing audience. For example, the paid listing generated by Query A from User A can be completely different from that produced from the same query made by User B. The factors that go into making this decision may include time of day, a differing historical profile, a different geo-targeting zone, or even demographic information that may be extracted from each user's profile. In effect, advertising messages can be custom-tailored with such granularity that each user's experience is unique.

Having all of this power at our disposal is something that can be simultaneously bracing and terrifying. Beyond the calculations required to serve up an optimized ad to each member of an ever-changing audience, each "ad unit" served may in fact be composed of hundreds of variables, and possibly hundreds of different creative elements. The accuracy of the calculations required to produce such customization has a direct impact on how much you will pay for a given advertising position, especially since the search engines reward marketers achieving higher Click-Through Rates than those whose ads do not perform as well.

How do you manage all of these complex variables? Although it's possible to run campaigns manually, either using the self-serve consoles of the search engines or via an external spreadsheet, because there are so many individual decisions that need to be made about each element constituting a search campaign, there are severe limitations to this approach. Having a technologically based solution in place is a necessity not only for the success of the campaign, but also for your own sanity.

Regardless of what technology solution you use—engine-supplied tools, rudimentary third-party bid management tools, or a more sophisticated platform—the importance of expertise and the human factor cannot be discounted. There needs to be a human in the loop somewhere: someone who understands your fundamental business objectives and who, at the end of the day, can review all the numbers and see if they really add up. Because so much of advertising and search marketing relies on the ability to hone marketing messages over time, experience and intelligence are absolute prerequisites to refining an existing campaign.

Even the engines understand that determining campaign structure—including how AdGroups (I'm referring to any engine's AdGroups) are populated, match types are selected, negative keywords are selected, and creativity is maximized—all still require the human touch. Larger advertisers may get some help from the search engines in these high-touch areas, but others will need to rely on their agencies or in-house teams. There's never any shortage of tactical to-do items in any campaign, so running campaigns and strategies is often a matter of prioritization.

6.3 Solutions: Build a Tech-Savvy Team

Many agencies running sophisticated digital marketing campaigns may be tempted to build large dedicated teams because many prospective clients have such a checkbox on their Requests for Proposal (RFPs), indicating that a dedicated team may be a selling point. But a large team, even a dedicated one, is meaningless if it isn't top notch, up to speed on the latest technologies, and professional in its execution of a project plan: it's not about a body count. Again, because this is not a hands-off, set-it-and-forget-it technology, digital marketing campaigns require not only the right technology, but also the right team of internal (and/or external) people for your business. As everyone's needs are different, it is imperative to always know what you need for your business and to keep track of what the engines are rolling out. More precise targeting and more ad formats (such as video, rich media, and audio) alone won't make your job easier.

Although humans and technology can often accomplish the same tasks, replacing technology with additional human resources is a mistake. There are notorious instances in which marketing teams have made agency selection choices based to a large extent on the requirement of a dedicated head count in the hope that there might be a superstar or two at the agency who would be redeployed to their account. That's a risky proposition, especially given some agencies' turnover. Additionally, whether or not there is a superstar in an agency, the use of that person in contract negotiations will not be limited to your company.

On the other hand, bid management serves as an example of people being almost fully replaced with technology. The search engines have provided tools to marketers who want to manage campaigns through the standard online interfaces. Much of the functionality that once was available only in third-party bid management solutions is now appearing in the Yahoo Panama interface (which was recently rolled out to advertisers), Google's AdWords, and Microsoft's adCenter. Better budget control and bid control are becoming standard engine-provided features, and the engines also offer third-party providers sophisticated APIs (Application Programming Interfaces) that allow for the execution of whatever formulaic campaign or bid strategies those third-party providers find appropriate.

But can these tasks be automated so technology is doing the heavy lifting, or is this a situation in which human experts need to watch and learn, applying creativity to challenges that an automated solution could never achieve? For most marketers, some combination of technology and people is optimal. The key is to select the right technology and the right team to manage, monitor, and deploy that technology.

Team Roles and Responsibilities

Currently, the advertising world has a shortage of search-engine-savvy tacticians and an even greater shortage of search-engine strategists. The technology is simply too new to yet have the staff needed by over 500,000 search advertisers. This shortage can make building an in-house team a daunting task, even if the team's primary function is to supervise external vendors (SEM agencies or technology companies). Realistically, you can't supervise a vendor if you don't know enough about their tasks and responsibilities to distinguish good from poor decisions or superb execution from mediocrity, which is why clients and prospects regularly request our help in recruiting in-house staff.

The skill sets and job categories involved with in-house search teams include:

1. SEM/SEO Copywriters.

Both paid and organic search are driven by language, linguistics, copy, and communication. Copywriters must be familiar with the nuances of organic SEO and understand paid search editorial guidelines and best practices. The copywriter must be taught to understand your business well enough to put himself in the searcher's shoes for every important listing. Often, ads with the highest CTR and ROI are fine-tuned by a copywriter. The best SEM copywriters think like newspaper headline writers: they understand that, in addition to including keywords, the ad should read like a newspaper headline—short, to the point, and relevant to the reader.

1. SEM/SEO Technologists.

Web marketing organizations have both organic and Pay-Per-Click (PPC) issues that benefit from implementing the right technology. An SEO technologist can make your site more spider-friendly by removing technological hurdles to the search engines' ability to find and understand all of the site's pages. Often, a technologist will prepare product feeds for Froogle or other shopping engines, such as Shopping.com, PriceGrabber.com, BizRate, and NexTag. An in-house or agency-side technology team will, of course, ensure all bidding activity in the search engines occurs as it should. For larger campaigns and those with volatile keywords, that means integration with the APIs at the engines.

2. Search Analysts and Paid Search Campaign Managers.

A well-managed PPC search campaign isn't static. Keywords and creativity are tested, and the campaign continually changes according to changing business needs. Various initiatives must be prioritized to ensure everything is executed properly and effectively. This requires the expertise of a search campaign manager.

3. Quant Jocks / Statisticians.

Good analysts understand the data and data drivers that may not be immediately obvious to those who aren't fluent with data analysis. A great analyst goes beyond that: he understands business. The best-run SEM campaigns often rely upon insight triggered by data review. Reporting and data are important for many reasons beyond communicating status reports to management, and data can and must be used to develop new strategic and tactical initiatives that test the current status quo against an alternate campaign execution. Recommended changes can occur anywhere within a campaign based on the reports available.

4. Web Master or External Conversion Marketer.

As high relevance and optimal conversion enable you to participate in the PPC auctions at the highest possible efficiency and scale, someone must be in charge of creating better user experiences for these power PPC keywords. It is unlikely your current site contains the perfect landing page for your most important keywords. Someone on your team should actively recommend and execute landing page creation and testing, as well as buy-flow or conversion-path analysis.

5. Strategists.

One or more people, in-house or at the agency, must see the big picture. The strategists understand the business's profit drivers and can make decisions regarding when to alter campaign objectives based on marketplace fluctuations, short-term business requirements, and competitive landscape.

6. SEM Agency Liaison (tactical level).

Many marketers choose to partially or fully outsource SEM. But even a fully outsourced PPC search campaign requires an internal person who shares responsibility for campaign aspects requiring client/advertiser involvement, such as landing-page testing, creative review, keyword approval, and data analysis/review. The best agency relationships are forged in a partnership environment.

All of these skill sets, roles, and functions are currently in high demand, and consequently, people qualified to perform them are hard to find and harder to keep. Take the time to educate yourself about the requirements of today's digital marketing, even if you plan to delegate the actual tasks to others (internally or externally).

In the meantime, use technology to automate as much as possible according to your campaign's makeup. Pull together a top-notch team internally as well as at your SEM agency (if you outsource), then focus on tactics and strategies that can make a difference. Always rally for the required internal and external resources because, if you correctly prioritize tactics, tests, and strategic initiatives, you'll progress.

CHAPTER 7

Fleeting Eyes
Change Is the Only Constant

"Every generation needs a new revolution."
—Thomas Jefferson

*

DIGITAL MARKETING is a fast-moving game. Today's top contenders for your ad dollars can easily become tomorrow's has-beens. Marketers face a constant battle to quickly identify new trends in order to capitalize on them, and the only constant seems to be the always surprising next hot opportunity to reach and influence consumers. Marketers must build and train teams, and develop a new ad strategy more quickly than ever, and this process will only continue to accelerate as additional new content platforms and advertising opportunities come into appearance and then reach critical mass. The problem for today's marketer is that by the time an opportunity reaches critical mass, it may be too late to fully capitalize on it.

7.1 Perils of Marketing to Fickle Audiences

The central problem that faces media companies and marketers as they attempt to monetize the millions of eyeballs attracted to mass niche sites such as MySpace and YouTube is how to do so without killing the golden goose. Any moves they make to better monetize these assets must be so subtle as to border on the invisible, or else their millions of users will defect. The current generation of heavy Web users aren't computer programmers, but they're more than equipped to quickly pull up stakes and transfer their friends and files to another service. Their only loyalty to a brand is function-based, and brands that no longer function for them—including MTV—have no place in their mediaverse. In other words, they're fickle, as youth has always been fickle: yesterday's overnight sensation is just one step away from being tomorrow's has-been joke, and this principle applies to multibillion-dollar brands as reliably as it does to Posh Spice or Britney Spears.

When Google bought YouTube and News Corp. bought Myspace, these corporations placed an enormous bet on these sites being able to somehow resist the inevitable tendency of dominant youth-oriented brands from being pulled into the abyss of generational irrelevancy within a comparatively short time frame. It took twenty years for MTV to become irrelevant, and it took youth-oriented sites such as GeoCities, TheGlobe, and Six Degrees perhaps five years to suffer the same fate.

Whether YouTube will follow the same trajectory is impossible to know, but unless Google and News Corp. walk a very fine line in their battle to monetize these sites, they'll muck up the particular magic that has brought them to their incredible critical mass.

Neither Google nor News Corp. is stupid, and each will likely resist making significant changes without considerable research. However, the problem with this cautious approach is that the numerous kids developing video/social networking sites, who are not constrained in this way, may, in the meantime, launch a competing service that's guaranteed to have a much higher "coolness factor," causing it to suddenly become the "in" place to hang out and self-publish. Again, given the fickle nature of youth, it's only a question of when, not whether, this will happen.

Making predictions about the future is dangerous, and placing bets on companies running Web media properties, because the whole world of media is becoming so incredibly unstable, is even more so. Users are inherently capricious and are always searching for the next coolest spot in which to hang out, watch and/or upload videos, chat, talk, and otherwise establish a virtual "nest." But these nests are temporary, and as soon as something better, faster, cheaper, or cooler comes along, these same users will be gone. And, as we all know, there are no real barriers to entry in this game: there are inspired people all over the world cobbling together Web-based applications aimed directly at the properties run by Fortune 100 companies, and these people don't care whether their targets are run by cool companies like Google or uncool companies like Fox. All they care about is building something cool, and, instead of going home at 5:00 p.m., they're working around the clock doing it. Many of them don't even care about whether these projects make money: they're just doing it for the thrill and peer prestige of crafting something that's great.

As marketers, we have to be aware that today's sure bet may be tomorrow's losing bet. We can't get comfortable with any marketing medium because that medium is quite likely to disappear or, in a "tragedy of the commons" scenario, become overloaded with competing marketers in the blink of an eye. What we can do, however, is closely watch what's happening, build nimble teams, and place our bets as sagaciously as we can with our advertising dollar, all the while knowing that all decisions are provisional in a dynamic marketplace. Still, the opportunities are so rich, and the potential so vast, that we gladly face the challenges of today's digital marketing environment, which more closely resembles whitewater rafting than piloting a steady ship on a calm sea.

7.2 Organic Search Results: An Endangered Species?

It's long been assumed as true among many Web users that the organic results served up by the search engines' algorithms are more relevant to most users' queries than the paid results. This perception has largely been manufactured by the search engines themselves, each of which seeks to endear itself to users as an "honest broker" whose neutral algorithms will unerringly separate the wheat from the chaff. Although the idea that organic results are "pure" is an inherently appealing one, in actuality the situation is much more complicated and, in many instances, paid listings actually provide better, more useful results than organic ones.

The first instance in which paid listings consistently provide more relevant results occurs when a user makes a query with local intent, for example, "plumber" or "office cleaning services." In this case, the search engine's ad server automatically geo-targets paid results that are based upon the user's IP address, which is mapped against a location database. So a user making such a search from New York will see paid listings for New York–based plumbers and janitors. Some engines are also supplementing the IP address geo-targeting with profile-based targeting by using user-volunteered data. This can also be accomplished with reasonable accuracy by watching a searcher's behavior over time and determining which geographies they select.

Organic listings, however, do not reflect the user's location unless the user types in an additional term to indicate one, such as "plumber NYC" or "plumber New York." Of course, that organic results aren't geo-targeted may not always produce less relevancy (if I'm researching the history of plumbing or whether plumbers in the United States belong to a union, I won't care about plumbers in my neighborhood). But for certain queries that clearly demonstrate a local intent, geo-targeted paid listings may deliver more relevancy than organic ones.

The second instance in which paid listings may provide better relevancy is more subtle, and it is a phenomenon caused by systemic structural biases affecting the way organic and paid listings are served. Organic results are, of course, subject to manipulation by wily SEO practitioners who are paid by their clients to secure the best ranking positions for their clients' sites. No one who practices SEO optimization likes to be labeled a cheater or manipulator, especially because many optimizers do provide a useful service to their clients by guiding them toward improving the search engine friendliness of their sites. But many of them will freely admit that they practice tricks and tactics that go beyond simple optimization into the zone of manipulation. For them, the ends (getting top rankings for their clients) justify whatever means they use to trick the engines into thinking that a given site is more relevant than it actually is.

The engines naturally seek to discourage such behavior, and do impose economic disincentives that constrain the optimizers' activities on an ad hoc basis. Severe penalties can be imposed when an optimizer crosses the line and gets caught, as we saw earlier this year when BMW.de and Ricoh.de were removed from Google's index for practicing deceptive tactics. The threat of these penalties does serve as a disincentive against extreme black-hat optimization tactics, but beyond this, it does nothing to enhance relevancy in the organic results space. As a rule, the more traffic that results-manipulation can get for the SEO types, the richer they will become, regardless of whatever negative impact on relevance such manipulation may have. And this irresistible economic reality is what drives the optimizers' behavior.

At the same time, a very different battle with its own set of economic rules is being waged among marketers running paid search campaigns. Here, each of these marketers seeks the highest possible SERP listings position at the lowest possible keyword acquisition price. Obviously, only one contestant can win this battle at any point in time, and bid price is only one factor determining the winner. Because the engines seek to maximize the number of clicks they sell, marketers serving ads that attract more clicks are rewarded with lower bid prices than those that don't (the exception is Yahoo, although it will very soon switch over to such a system). In a nutshell, the engines' auctions provide powerful economic incentives for marketers to produce the most compelling, most likely-to-be-clicked-upon, most relevant results. That this result, which maximizes the engines' revenues, happens to accord with users' desire for relevancy, is one of the happier coincidences in the search-marketing industry.

Another factor enforcing relevancy in the paid search marketplace is that marketers are penalized for attracting irrelevant traffic. Ironically, marketers seeking to advertise with irrelevant terms or with less than relevant creativity are often attracting traffic less likely to convert. For example, if you work for a law firm that specializes in civil practice, you would not want people looking for criminal defense attorneys to click on your ad. So it would be foolhardy to bid highly to gain top rankings for the term "lawyer" because you'd be wasting tens, perhaps hundreds of dollars each day paying the engines for clicks of which a high percentage will never convert. Those nonconverting visitors wasted your money and their own time. Consequently, the search engines have established a system rewarding relevance in the PPC search results in order to keep their searchers happy and clicking.

On the other hand, if your firm happened to have high organic rankings for the term "lawyer," you wouldn't really mind if 75 percent of your clicks came from people seeking criminal defense attorneys. Nor would you take any steps to deoptimize your site to decrease the inbound traffic, even though most of it will never convert. After all, organic traffic is free (once you get the position with or without SEO help).

Consequently, two very different sets of incentives and disincentives operate to determine the production of organic and paid search results. One is biased toward relevancy, and the other forces the search engine to proactively fight to maintain relevancy pitted against an army of web masters and SEO practitioners all of whom want that "free" top spot for their favorite keywords. While it is true that top-ranking organic results are rarely totally irrelevant, SEOs can game the system easily enough to manufacture a sense of relevancy that is in fact a phantom. Because there are no built-in penalties for doing so (except when one crosses the line and is caught), this practice is rampant and degrades the relevancy of organic results.

With paid search, we have exactly the opposite situation: marketers are rewarded for enhancing relevancy—not degrading it—which enhances the relevancy of paid results. Although it's true that a marketer who cares only about traffic—and not about conversions or ROI—could run ads irrelevant to a user's queries in an attempt to cast a wide net, such a marketer would pay an enormous penalty. For this reason, few marketers engage in this behavior. Even marketers looking to build brand by using paid search will get more for their dollar if their content is relevant and engaging. And as the search engines evolve their strategies for battling falsely inflated organic results, due to the inevitable operation of these opposing economic systems across the behavior of thousands of marketers, it is likely this phenomenon will only increase.

7.3 The PC-Browser-SERP Paradigm Is Not Immutable

Search marketing is fundamentally simple. All marketers realize they need to place messages that most closely relate to a user's query in both relevance and position. What makes the process complex is that SERPs provide for more than one message to be placed, and a real-time auction allocates position based on bid. Additionally, in hybrid auctions (systems that the three major engines are already running), various scoring mechanisms influence the bid price. Although each search engine's organic and ad-serving algorithms differ significantly, fundamentally they all share remarkably common features, beginning with the SERP. While the presentation of these "answer" pages differs noticeably, at root they contain the same two main content components: organic results and sponsored results.

The SERP paradigm of multiple results, however, is neither eternal nor immutable, and it quickly disentegrates as the search bar relocates itself from the browser/searcher/clicker model toward other platforms in which the central query/response mechanism will continue to be central. The most obvious example of this is seen in mobile cell phone browsers, in which the 1024 x 768 browser window is reduced to a tiny fraction of a monitor's screen size. Text size must be proportionally expanded to be readable on these tiny screens, which naturally reduces the number of results, either organic or sponsored, that can be displayed per any given query. The use of mobile cell phone browsers will continue to reinforce the pressure on marketers to achieve top-ranked positions, especially as the cost of not being number one is far steeper on a cell phone than it is on a computer monitor.

The search engines are naturally interested in extending their self-serve ad platforms to the cell phone in order to extend their reach. In early September 2006, Google began allowing its AdWords marketers to create mobile ads for cellular carriers in Germany (T-Mobile, Vodafone, E-Plus, O2), the United Kingdom (T-Mobile, Vodafone, O2, Orange), and the United States (Cingular, Sprint, Verizon, T-Mobile, Nextel). Yahoo has been providing search services since early 2005 for Nokia, and Microsoft's clear interest in extending adCenter to non-Web search platforms was demonstrated when it announced that a cell phone add-on to its soon-to-be-introduced Zune MP3 music player is in the works.

What's been so far missing from the equation is the kind of critical mass of users and marketers capable of creating an actual marketplace. The number of G3 cell phone users in the United States is still comparatively small, and only about 10 million people are capable of being exposed to mobile search marketing messages. But industry analysts have forecast robust growth for mobile marketing: mobile industry watcher Informa predicts $1.7 billion in revenues for 2007 that will ramp up to $11 billion by 2011.

What remains to be seen is whether the carriers will submit to the search engines' desires to extend their empires beyond the pay-as-you-go, bring-your-own-bandwidth Internet. Cell carriers "own" the pipes (or at least the frequencies), and they naturally want to maximize their share of any ad revenues derived from mobile search. Some carriers have clearly articulated that, instead of cutting Google, Yahoo, or Microsoft in on the ad pie, they intend to manage their own ad networks.

Regardless of how these issues sort out, as a marketer, you need to be watching the mobile market carefully, and you need to be prepared to take advantage of it sooner rather than later. Many of us in the search-engine market reminisce fondly of the "old days" of PPC, when competition was less steep, click prices were lower, and ROI easier to gain. The same benefits of being an early adopter will likely accrue to mobile search marketers.

The bad news, of course, is that the addition of mobile search capabilities will further complicate the management of your existing and future paid search campaigns. Make sure your in-house team or SEM agency is current on this new platform and able to create or adopt your existing search campaigns to maximally leverage it.

7.4 New Digital Channels Will Have Different Marketing Potentials

Few expect today's traditional computing paradigm—the desktop box, the keyboard, and the monitor—to continue its traditional dominance much longer. We are quickly approaching a time when the primary computing device will be small, portable, and quite possibly wearable. This device will seamlessly and wirelessly connect with an array of peripheral equipment.

The voice carriers, AT&T/Cingular, Verizon, Sprint, and others, have declared their intention to be players in whatever advertising platform evolves on mobile devices. So have the search engines, each of which plans to extend their ad platforms to the cell phone.

Many details about how these ad platforms will work are still unclear. As it is doubtful that people using such devices will tap in commands via a keyboard, information requests may use a voice interface, in which case both queries and answers will be processed by voice. But voice communication is linear and sequential, imposing the requirement that advertising attached to it be sequential and, quite necessarily, interruptive. And it is unlikely that consumers would be willing to stand for voice commercials interrupting the flow of their queries and answers. Instead, they will want immediate results, and will likely resist any attempted interruptions from marketers.

That mobile advertising may allow marketers to exploit localization technologies in order to notify a given user, for example, that the restaurant he's walking by has a special on steak sandwiches has generated a great deal of discussion. This possibility prompts questions such as, how can such a system be smart enough to suppress such advertising if the cell phone user is a vegetarian? For this kind of intelligence to be innate within any such system, much more would have to be known about the user than his simple geographical location. Instead, the ability to link location data to historical search query data, voluntarily submitted self-disclosures, and otherwise tap into his digital footprint would be a tool of much greater value to marketers.

Whoever connects these elements will be able to exert considerable control over the next evolution of digital advertising as it moves into the mobile arena. Although mobile carriers will want to be key players in this marketplace, whether they have the ability to integrate the intelligence necessary to make such mobile advertising work remains to be seen. Instead, it is likely that a partnership between carriers and the search engines, which already possess terabytes of information relating to the individual predilections of their customers, will provide the infrastructure for such next-generation mobile advertising platforms.

We believe that, as most mobile devices will dial a number when the browser cursor is positioned over it and clicked, one valid form of paid mobile advertising will be pay-per-call. Given the mobile user's likely objectives when conducting a search, this form of monetization may be a better fit than pay-per-click.

7.5 Digital Marketing: Too Powerful to Be Left Alone?

The better the targeting tools become and the closer marketers are able to track their customers who leave permanent trails behind their every online move, the more the issue of privacy will threaten even the best-laid marketing plan. Consumer privacy advocates may not represent the majority of consumers, but they do tend to be vocal, particularly toward the government.

In 2006 this issue became heated several times, though it never actually caused lawmakers to pass new legislation regulating the marketing industry. By far the most notable event was AOL's data breach, which made the search queries of 650,000 AOL users public without their consent.

But the AOL data breach was just the beginning. Facebook users came to the unpleasant realization that the site's new Real Simple Syndication (RSS) feed managed to broadcast personal events (such as breaking up a relationship) to people they didn't know. More than half a million players of Second Life, a popular online virtual reality game, had their personal data, including real names and addresses, stolen by a hacker. Computer giant Hewlett-Packard became embroiled in a lurid privacy scandal involving "pretexting" that caused its chairwoman to step down and may result in jail time for some other participants. And in a truly bizarre incident on Craigslist, a self-described "prankster" impersonated a woman seeking sexual partners. After receiving more than 150 e-mail responses, he "outed" the responders—some of whose messages contained revealing photos and personal identification details—by posting all the e-mails on a public web site.

Every day, it seems, there's a new data leak or privacy breach. Each time this happens, users' trust in the institution we call the Internet drops a notch, and when marketers are implicated in these breaches, trust in online marketing takes a hit. Users are increasingly seeking to guard personal data, including search query data. A new breed of tools such as TrackMeNot and Lost in the Crowd, which mask user queries from search engines by firing out "junk queries," are one approach. Other users delete their cookies, or otherwise seek to cloak their identities using various anonymizing programs. These reactions are not only understandable, given how insecure personal information is on the Net, they're quite rational.

These stories of data breaches and personal privacy have little to do with search-engine marketing or the ability of marketers to target advertising based on anonymous cookie profile data. The press, however, may fail to draw a distinction between personally identifiable profiles and nonpersonally identifiable profile data.

Marketers walk a fine line through this minefield. Search marketers, a part of the vanguard of the targeting revolution, need to pay special attention to the privacy issue. Search engines, SEM agencies, and Behavioral Targeting (BT) technology researchers and vendors all have access to extensive query and user databases that enable us to create efficient, ROI-positive and market-share building search campaigns.

We all seek competitive advantage, which means knowing more about users and prospects than other marketers. We all welcome the new generation of targeting technologies that allows us to analyze the click stream and historical user behavior in order to present the best and most relevant ad at the most opportune time. But we also know that if these technologies become overly obtrusive, or if data is shared or released in a way that allows individuals to be identified, we risk causing a user backlash that can set our industry back by either making it less efficient or, worse, subject to government regulations. There are those in the U.S. government who "hear there's rumors on the Internets" or "it's a series of tubes" and may pass legislation significantly affecting an industry they don't adequately understand. And, internationally, the situation is similar.

At the same time, as long as the line between marketing intelligence and actual spying isn't crossed, most users show a remarkable willingness to allow marketers entry to their profile data. Because they want access to free, ad-supported content and services, they are willing to divulge personal information. But no one wants personal data aggregated in a way that encourages spamming or stalking, or allows wholesale data releases, such as the AOL fiasco, which make their most intimate query data public information. These concerns are not idle ones; in mid-2006, Arizona authorities arrested Heather Kane, a woman who ordered a murder hit on a woman who had become a "Myspace Friend" of her boyfriend's.

So far, the search engines have brushed aside suggestions that, because they retain user query data indefinitely, each is sitting on top of a privacy time bomb. Each has provided multiple assurances that this data is secure, but each also refuses to discuss the steps it takes to ensure that releases of this data are impossible (in a peculiar way, their stances reflect the posture of the U.S. government, which has admitted that it has multiple electronic surveillance programs in place, but cannot discuss them because to do so would place in danger of attack from our enemies). Google has taken a tough stance against sharing this data with the U.S. government but, in early September, agreed to share data about its Orkut users with Brazilian authorities. Whether Google will be able to withstand similar inquiries from the U.S. government, especially where national security is implicated by a particular user's search behavior, remains to be seen.

The interactive advertising industry has long understood the fine line between marketing intelligence and spying, and has taken what steps it can: the IAB publishes privacy guidelines to which all members must adhere (http://www.iab.net/standards/privacy.asp). Most reputable commercial sites have privacy policies, but the real issue isn't policy, but rather execution, and this is where we have much room for improvement.

7.6 Solutions: Guard Your Data

How do you handle the data flowing through your servers? How tightly do you control its dissemination? What policies are in place to prevent its distribution—inadvertent or intentional—to third parties? What policies do your third-party contractors, including your digital marketing agency, abide by? All of these questions need to be answered now, while your data is safeguarded, not after an unauthorized data release. By then it will be too late to shield your organization from civil—and perhaps even criminal—liability.

And if you have any doubt whether the U.S. federal government intends to have a vote in the development of our new era of targeting, take note of the FTC's recent $1 million fine against social networking site Xanga, which improperly handled its users' personal information. Ironically, through the effort to protect the privacy of individuals, the government and even the industry may also sacrifice the improved ad targeting and user experience that results from the retention of anonymous data (non–Personally Identifiable data). Let's hope a balance is found that allows search marketing to heighten users' experience without risking their privacy and trust. Unfortunately, if another breach occurs, it may be followed by restrictive legislation that will impose mandatory rules on how search marketing is conducted, which is not something I would like to avoid. However, if marketers can't ensure the safety of users' data, the federal government will.

7.7 Solutions: You Need a Translator

The new media forms that will achieve dominance in the next few years will all be eminently measurable. Because they eliminate any need to question whether your marketing dollars were or were not effective, this measurability will provide their essential selling point. You'll be able to see exactly what your dollars are doing for you, and that's both an incredible strength and an incredible problem.

Why is it a problem? Since your marketing objectives are big, in the age of digital marketing the mechanisms to achieve them require thousands of micro-decisions occurring at the tactical level. Although all of these tactical decisions need to be aligned with your marketing objectives, none in themselves are significant enough to warrant the attention of a CMO.

A translator breaks down the macro goals into their constituent parts, makes them executable, and translates the results back into decisions that a CMO or other executive can understand, review, and act upon. This translation function is essential because, without it, executive-level marketers run the risk of spending all their time making tactical decisions, which necessarily draws them away from their proper and necessary strategic role.

Having access to a technology platform capable of managing the thousands of tactical decisions required to run digital marketing campaigns is a necessary but insufficient condition for success. But the essential translation function cannot be achieved by a machine alone. There needs to also be human intelligence that analyzes the reporting data and then makes it actionable.

As the world increasingly moves beyond mass buys on dumb networks to smart buys on ever more tightly segmented and targeted smart networks, the importance of translation grows more critical. Without translators and analysts, the flow of numbers from measurable media forms becomes an unintelligent torrent of babble that cannot understood, much less acted upon. Unless this data can be processed by managers into a form that relates to a marketer's macro-level goals, it's worthless. It is a translator who gives this data its objective worth.

Integrating one's various marketing efforts—offline, online, and through targeted digital marketing such as search—offers another considerable challenge. Anecdotal evidence suggests that the development of any kind of integrated platform capable of managing these disparate elements is a distant possibility. One vendor of media buying integration software suggested that 50 percent of Fortune 500 companies perform analyses of the effectiveness of these efforts "by hand" (http://www.imediaconnectoin.com/content/8922.asp). The backwardness of the process of buying media stands in stark contrast to the generally high level of automation and integrated systems in the modern corporation, and this process needs extensive reform. On the other side of this coin, however, the antiquated systems and processes of the ad industry also pose tremendous opportunities for those who are capable of reengineering it.

7.8 Solutions: If You Can't Do This Work In-house, Outsource It

If you lack the internal resources to carry out effective search campaigns, outsourcing digital marketing may make sense for your business. The best digital marketing agencies provide many valuable services, including extensive consultations regarding your business goals, a highly customized campaign, frequent reporting, and a measurably higher ROI than what would be possible from an in-house digital marketing campaign. Agencies usually work on percentage of media spend, which will very likely be justified by the increase of profits realized through more efficient campaigns.

However impatient you may be to dive into search, make sure you are prepared to make an educated decision about a digital agency before contracting. Here are a few things to look for:

1. Technology.

When running search-based digital marketing campaigns, most agencies use automated-bid management software and campaign management technology. Ask some tough questions: Was the technology built in-house or acquired off the shelf from a third-party vendor? How suited is it to the way you run your business? How easily can it be customized? How often is it upgraded? How much training does the agency provide for its staff to operate it? Sadly, a lot of agencies don't invest much in their technology infrastructure, either in training or in the all-important ability to tailor its operation in order to provide for their clients needs. Marketers who know what they are trying to accomplish with any technology are in a much stronger position to make a good decision. The savvy marketer does not let a vendor sell based on sizzle. Whether selecting web-analytics or a campaign management platform, it is key to match the vendor against your specific business objectives that have been determined and outlined ahead of time.

2. Client Services.

How does the agency organize its client services department? Who's in charge of it? What level of prior client services experience does he or she have? Does their client services team have the knowledge and resources needed to manage your campaign? Can the team escalate questions to the experts and company founders? Naturally, the more you're spending, the more likely it will be that the agency will prioritize your campaign and assign a more senior team accordingly, but even modest spenders deserve a high level of responsiveness and customer care even if the account manager doesn't know every answer off the top of her head.

3. Industry Reputation.

Entering the digital agency business is not difficult, and as a result, many people have been starting their own agencies for years. In order to make an informed decision about the professional background of the agency, be sure to research the agency executives. Google them and see what they've written on industry topics. Examine their philosophies, recommendations, and command of the search landscape. Take note of their presence (or lack thereof) at major industry conferences. With which professional associations does the agency hold membership? How well did the agency perform in "agency shoot-outs," such as those conducted by Jupiter Research? Do the agency executives have strong contacts at the engines from the executive level on down? The more you know about those at the helm of a given agency, the more informed your decision will be.

Lastly, there's no better determinant of agency excellence than in-person recommendations. You're not going to buy a $50 product on Amazon without reading customer reviews, So don't make the imperative agency decision without performing and even higher level of due diligence. However, as you probably are aware, every SEM— the good and the bad—has a couple of good references (perhaps their clueless clients), which is why Jupiter Research relies on feedback from a diversity of customers when releasing the SEM Agency

Constellation reports. Be sure to investigate all aspects of an agency's past performance.

There's no reason you should be saddled with an underperforming agency, and there's nothing wrong with being demanding. Your loyalty should be to your shareholders and stakeholders, not your agency. There are many good agencies out there, and if you perform a reasonable level of due diligence, you can be confident your experience with the agency of your choice will be happy and extremely productive.

CHAPTER 8

Eyes on the Prize

Assessing the Digital Marketing Opportunities Provided by Today's Major Players

"It is not the strongest of the species that survive, nor the most intelligent, but the one most responsive to change."

—Charles Darwin

*

THE MAJOR search engines have evolved beyond publishers, transforming themselves into digital marketplaces whose features differ markedly. Each compete vigorously to attract the interest of users and marketers by constantly introducing new products and features. Each is also a media network extending its tentacles into publishers (and even broadcasters) and providing those publishers a new revenue stream. While Google, which commands approximately 50 percent of worldwide search query volume, is the clear leader, both Yahoo and Microsoft possess both the intent and the capabilities to gain market share in the years ahead, provided they can deploy products and services that can best serve marketplace stakeholders, including consumers, advertisers, and publishers/broadcasters. At the same time, new players—especially mobile carriers, content owners and even governments—will begin to exert more control over how these marketplaces operate. Technology-driven innovation in advertising will continue to accelerate, having already produced a group of companies that are deploying alternative advertising marketplaces, streamlining the production of creative assets, and improving ad targeting for both on- and offline advertising channels.

It is difficult to resist the temptation to say something oracular about the prospects of the three major search engines that dominate today's digital-marketing landscape: Google, Yahoo, and Microsoft. With the proviso that this landscape is too dynamic to provide accurate long-term predictions, there are certain observations that can be stated about how each search engine has historically run its marketplace, the philosophies that have supported its growth, and the technologies that might enable it to continue to prosper. With paid search not even ten years old, there will be dramatic additional evolution in the next five to ten years.

This discussion should not be interpreted as advice to marketers to rely exclusively on any one of these engines. Instead, it is always best to spread your money around to where you are likely to find an audience that is most apt to operate, be it on search engines or elsewhere in the thousands of digital nooks.

8.1 Google

Google's first-mover advantage, which paved the way by developing a useful, attractive search engine supported by an efficient, CPC-based ad system, positioned it as a market leader. But its real strength is its singular focus on search, a philosophy that runs through everything it does, from its sparse and lean home page (which has consistently resisted multiple pressures to "portalize" it) to its insistence that everything it does is aimed at a very simple proposition: to provide the best experience for its users. Another factor that Google has leveraged to its advantage is its culture, which encourages the development of early-stage technologies—the vast majority of which will likely never result in commercially viable products or services. This culture, which eschews hierarchical structures in favor of a flat one, has been criticized as being overly chaotic, and it is likely that its various product missteps are a direct result of this chaos. But as long as Google adheres to its overall corporate goal of improving and perhaps even perfecting the user experience in search, its execution will likely remain a very hard mark to best. Simply put, Google understands that without the loyalty of its users, it has nothing, and it will zealously protect this relationship against attempts to compromise its excellence.

Google's users, of course, are not the only constituents to contributed to its enormous success. Without the willingness of advertisers to participate in its digital marketplace, Google would just be another interesting company with some interesting technology. In regard to its relationship with advertisers, Google has not demonstrated the same level of commitment to guiding marketers through its complex and arcane methods of running its marketplace as it has with its users. Its critics have characterized Google's stance toward resolving complaints from advertisers as arrogant, unfeeling, and similar to the same imperious old media networks it challenges. Furthermore, as long as demand for position within Google's SERPs exceeds the supply, Google probably does not need to concern itself with providing the equivalent level of care and service as it does for its end-users. As we saw in Chapter 4, however, the degree of advertiser unhappiness is not just a PR problem for Google. Unless addressed properly, these issues can grow to such widespread unhappiness that marketers, at the very least, will welcome an alternative that is more advertiser friendly and less likely to be perceived as arrogant.

Google's history of innovation, large market cap ($152 billion, as of this writing), and clear intention to extend its self-serve ad platform into nonsearch media will continue to make it a formidable competitor as well as a primary destination for digital marketers. In May 2007,

Google flexed its financial muscles when it announced plans to acquire DoubleClick, an online advertising company, for $3.1 billion. The acquisition of DoubleClick, the dominant server of graphical display advertising on the Web, will significantly extend the range and depth of data available to Google for targeted advertising purposes. Yet it is this very prospect that alarmed industry competitors such as Microsoft, which immediately called upon the U.S. Justice Department and Federal Trade Commission, which both share antitrust monitoring duties, to examine the acquisition.

Privacy advocates, including the Center for Digital Democracy and the Electronic Privacy Information Center, also joined the fray, noting that a combined enterprise of Google's policy of gathering and retaining its users search query data for an unlimited period of time and DoubleClick's ability to precisely track the Web-surfing of millions) would pose substantial risks to user privacy. Both companies issued statements intended to assure the public and regulatory bodies that no such risk existed. DoubleClick's statement noted that

> information collected by DoubleClick DART ad serving technology belongs to DoubleClick's clients and not to DoubleClick. Any and all information collected by DoubleClick is, and will remain, the property of the company's clients [and that such] ownership rights [would be unaffected by any acquisition].

These statements may have assured some, but they left unanswered the larger and more difficult questions of the rights that consumers—users—can exert over the data that such organizations collect. Does data on your Web-surfing habits, collected by DoubleClick, belong to Proctor & Gamble? To GM? Or to you? Because Google depends on the continuing good will of its users, who continue to reward it with the lion's share of search query volume, these questions are critical. As of this writing, the Google-DoubleClick acquisition has been referred to the Federal Trade Commission as part of a formal inquiry.

As the digital ad marketplace matures, Google's place in it will continue to evolve. If Google succeeds in simultaneously broadening its online reach and also bridging the chasm to offline media, they will have a compelling value proposition. The advantage of being able to use one integrated platform for the delivery of advertising across multiple digital channels represents real value to marketers, both by simplifying the campaign planning and creative process and by providing integrated reporting that will allow marketers to evaluate and refine their digital marketing campaigns in real-time fashion. However, unless they become a full media monopoly, there will still be a need for third-party agencies and technologies to aggregate Google-controlled media data with that of other media so that the right media mix decisions can be made by an independent third party.

8.2 Yahoo

Yahoo represents an interesting case of a property that successfully evolved from a directory into a portal, and now (with its purchase of Overture) comprises not only one of the Web's preeminent destination sites but also a mature advertising platform. Unlike Google, which has both positioned itself as and behaved like a classic, engineer-driven technology company, Yahoo has historically preferred to refer to itself as a "media company." Its expansion has been based on acquiring and aggregating as many related properties as possible in order to create user loyalty inspired not by excelling in one thing, but rather by providing a broad array of services designed to aggregate as large an audience as possible. Its growth posture represents only a slight evolution of the "sticky portal" strategy embarked upon by so many large-content sites of the late 1990s.

Without attempting to minimize Yahoo's technological prowess, its approach to technology has always been more "buy" than "build." Up until comparatively recently, search was an outsourced process, and only since 2002 and 2003, when it acquired Inktomi, Overture, and AltaVista, has Yahoo developed in-house technological capabilities making its offerings functionally equal to Google.

In 2006, Yahoo had a rough year. Its comparative inabilities to monetize its search inventory became apparent, but it was able to launch its next-generation Panama platform successfully. While it is too early to ascertain the degree to which Panama will pull marketing dollars from Google or match Google's monetization rate, this successful deployment bodes well for Yahoo's future because it will more effectively monetize Yahoo's search inventory. To marketers, the downside of Panama is clear: before, Yahoo's search marketplace had used a straight auction that did not factor in performance, but it is now as opaque as Google's, limiting the control and transparency that marketers have previously used to their advantage.

While Google remains the place for marketers to achieve scale, Yahoo's assets translate into viable inventory opportunities for marketers. Yahoo has a capable behavioral ad-targeting product called Impulse, which allows display advertising to be served across the Yahoo network based upon behavioral profile data, including search behavior. Yahoo, thanks to its acquisition of so many properties over the years, and those that it has built itself, also has a large inventory pool under direct control.

In October 2006, Yahoo acquired a 20 percent stake in online media exchange RightMedia; in April 2007, it purchased the remaining 80 percent for $680 million. RightMedia, a network of networks, will allow Yahoo to both buy and sell remnant inventory in an automated fashion. Although RightMedia is growing rapidly, it has competition, notably from DoubleClick, which seems destined to become part of Google's online ad empire.

While Yahoo appears to be fighting a losing battle with Google for raw traffic, it is by far too early to declare this battle over—or even half begun. If Yahoo can serve advertisers with the right mix of media options in the right way, it will once again gain the respect of both advertisers and Wall Street.

8.3 Microsoft

Whereas Google and Yahoo share the common characteristic of companies formed in order to exploit traffic on the World Wide Web, Microsoft was conceived as a vendor of operating systems, applications, and, only much later, content. Only in the mid-1990s did it foresee that the advent of the World Wide Web posed a serious enough challenge to its cash-cow operating system business to warrant a response. Its main response was to attack Netscape, whose Navigator browser was the de facto standard for accessing the Web. In doing so, Microsoft waged a war that eventually made it the subject of an antitrust suit, but ultimately gave it dominance in terms of browser software. Microsoft, like Yahoo, used its financial leverage to begin acquiring Web content companies, notably Hotmail, through joint ventures, such as MSNBC.com, along with the deployment of a national dial-up network, the Microsoft Network.

Today, Microsoft's management is aware that Google's growing financial power and growing dominance over search advertising revenues is an enormous threat to Microsoft's empire. Google, for its part, has launched an array of products—from word processors to spreadsheets—intended to draw users away from Microsoft's application software suite. If history is any judge, Microsoft will leverage its traditional dominance over client software to steer users to its own competing search service, but, given that it remains under governmental oversight, Microsoft will not use the same tactics it used against Netscape in the mid-1990s.

Microsoft has invested considerable sums in developing a competing search service as well as a PPC-based ad auction service called adCenter, which formerly launched in early 2006. Microsoft's adCenter, which included advanced geo- and demographic-targeting capabilities for Microsoft Search, raised the bar in providing advanced targeting technology for marketers. While Microsoft's share of search query volume remains a small fraction of Google's (their percent query share is in the low teens), the benefits of having a deep-pocketed company like Microsoft make such investments in targeted advertising technologies extend past the users of adCenter. Given the fierce rivalry that will certainly continue in the next few years, the competition between Google and Microsoft will prove beneficial to marketers, whose loyalty will never be to a particular search engine but rather to whoever can build a marketplace that allows them the greatest flexibility and return on investment. So far, Microsoft has demonstrated that it is serious about constructing an advertiser-friendly platform, and was the first to introduce such features as demographic targeting, using profile data harvested from Hotmail and other popular properties that use user-supplied registration data.

Recently, Microsoft has demonstrated a newfound willingness to pay large amounts in order to acquire strategic pieces that it lacks in the online advertising puzzle. In May 2007, just a few weeks after Google announced its plan to acquire DoubleClick, Microsoft announced that it would buy aQuantive, a company with a successful interactive ad agency (Avenue A/Razorfish), a set of widely used tools for buying and selling online advertising (Atlas DMT), and an ad-brokering network (Drive PM), for $6 billion. While it remains to be seen whether Microsoft will retain or dispose of the ad agency portion of aQuantive, the ability to integrate Atlas DMT within adCenter will extend adCenter's reach, giving Microsoft a powerful boost in its attempt to build a digital marketplace that is large and sophisticated enough to challenge Google. Ironically, although opposing some of Google's potential opportunities for abusive market power, Microsoft may need to address several conflicts of interest if it chooses to retain the agency portion of aQuantive, Avenue A/Razorfish. The agency community competing with Avenue A/Razorfish, although placing media dollars with Microsoft, may see a true conflict. Similarly, the clients of Avenue A/Razorfish who rely upon their agency to impartially steward their media dollars may be concerned about the "mothership" being awarded preference when several competing media opportunities have similar likelihoods of success.

Microsoft is also a leader in exploring the advertising possibilities inherent in gaming, which is projected to be among the fastest-growing fields in digital marketing in the years ahead. In May 2006, it purchased Massive, a company specializing in the dynamic placement of advertising messages within video games. The market for advertising within such games is projected to grow to $2.5 billion per year by 2010, and represents a way to reach the choice eighteen-to-thirty-four demographic in a way that pioneers new ground in contextual placement.

Microsoft has also positioned itself to be a strong player in IPTV (Internet Protocol Television), and is now working with sixteen cable networks worldwide in order to provide tools and solutions for this next-generational interactive television platform. IPTV systems provide a range of popular services, including Video-on-Demand, Digital Video Recording, multiple simultaneous PIP (Picture in Picture) displays, and other interactive features. For marketers and advertisers, IPTV systems represent a current platform for a new generation of targeted video marketing, wherein each user in a cable network is consuming a unique stream of video content.

Although Microsoft can no longer consider itself as nimble as a newly minted startup, there are thousands of extremely bright people working at Microsoft, and the challenge of having a fierce rival in Google may be just what the company needs to reinvigorate itself.

8.4 Other Players to Watch

It is natural, given Google's dominance in the current digital marketplace (plus its stated intention to extend its successful self-serve, performance-based ad platform to nonsearch media), to focus exclusively on Google's battle for marketplace preeminence against players vying for the same customers, which overwhelmingly access the Internet's vast resources through the PC-browser-based method. But it is likely that the advertising paradigm will have to change radically as new forms of accessing information emerge, including the use of mobile devices. These devices impose their own requirements and constraints on the forms that advertising must take. Although Google, Yahoo, Microsoft, and the other engines would like to extend their hegemony to this new computing paradigm, there are other players who are unlikely to give up their toll-taking roles on these new wireless channels without a fight.

Wireless carriers, over whose networks an increasing share of digital traffic will flow, will have a voice in how future ad marketplaces work, and the world over which they exert control is quite different from the one that the existing players operate. Devices operating over wireless networks do not require an operating system produced by Microsoft, nor do they require communications functions or content supplied by Google or Yahoo. Wireless operators can buy or develop any technologies they need because they control access to those users that every one wants. Because they are the gatekeepers to hundreds of millions of eyes and ears, they can set the rules.

On January 2, 2007, AT&T announced that advertising would be the centerpiece of its new wireless strategy, and that it had built a sales force to sell advertising to reach the 58.7 million subscribers belonging to its Cingular wireless network. Its CEO stated that this opportunity represented one amounting to "several billion dollars per year" (Reported in Media Post Daily News, 01/02/06, http://publications.mediapost.com/ index.cfm?fuseaction=Articles.showArticleHomePage&art_aid=53228). In doing so, AT&T joined Verizon, which less than a week before had announced it would begin to sell advertisements to reach its 57 million-member network, and Sprint, a network of 51 million, which announced in October it would do the same.

When you add up all the numbers, that's a lot of eyeballs.

Offline Media Marketplaces

Many online media opportunities are perfect for the network model being developed and perfected by both the search engines as well as other ad networks such as Advertising.com, ValueClick, Tribal Fusion, Casale Media Network, BlueLithium, Burst Media, Vibrant Media, Undertone Networks, AdBrite, and Federated Media. A new ad network hawking either specialized or nondifferentiated online media seems to pop up every day; at every trade show new entrants are making their pitch with booths and swarms of young, enthusiastic, freshly minted grads.

In the offline world and within search, it has been proven that auctions of valuable assets generally result in far higher prices when there is agreement among bidders as to the value of the asset being auctioned. This lack of transparency, coupled with a failure of the auction network to communicate the value of their inventory, led to failures of those 1990s auction marketplaces and dismal participation by marketers in the Google print media tests. For offline and future online auctions to succeed, each auction must be accompanied by key foundational data about the media placement being auctioned. For most advertising placements, that information would be targeting parameters, such as context, behavior, age, gender, geography, etc. Of course, some media buyers also need to account for additional factors such as daypart, placement within the medium, and how well the medium will integrate the creative ad unit the advertiser wishes to run. Then there are the intangibles: How much would advertisers pay for *Drive Time Howard Stern* spots if the auction closed the night before at midnight Eastern Time?

Some attributes associated with particular media placements are difficult to define so that the advertiser understands the uniqueness of the placement and the publisher gets full value. Consequently, some media will not be auctioned within a network-style marketplace. Special media placements require discrete auction marketplaces like eBay, which allow the seller to describe easily each placement's intrinsic value. If properly defined, and with a reasonable number of advertisers participating in the discrete marketplace, an auction always results in higher yield than a negotiated price. This is why pork bellies, oil, gold, and FCOJ are sold this way, as well as currencies, stocks, and bonds.

The eBay Opportunity

There are several players vying for the top spot as auction house for the discrete sale of well-defined media assets in a nonnetwork environment (media placements are not mixed). With a $50 million test of a TV media auction in conjunction with a coalition of advertisers who have positioned the auction as a way for broadcasters to unload inventory (presumably with advertisers buying that inventory inexpensively), eBay is at the forefront. However, marketers and advertisers needn't be in too much of a rush to create frictionless transparent marketplaces for media assets—although publishers, on the other hand, should. The eBay experiment is at risk because from the start it has been mispositioned as a discount auction for remnant space. As an auction platform for discrete media, It has a tremendous amount going for it, not the least of which includes:

- trusted brand for auctions
- ability to specify an XML or other semantic scheme to allow auction participants to properly describe every media placement being auctioned
- strong API and Web services competence and expertise
- payment platform for clearing small- to mid-size purchases

The original trial URL for eBay's media marketplace was admarketpilot.com. Interestingly, that domain registration has not been renewed and is scheduled to lapse by the time this book hits store shelves. eBay recently switched to www.ebaymediamarketplace.com—a more fitting name for a media marketplace.

There are other players looking to make their mark as online media exchanges for offline media assets. One is SoftWave Media Exchange (www.swmx.com), which specializes in providing targeted media buys for radio and TV. SWMX's services, which are activated and monitored through a Web-based front-end, include automated spot delivery, account reconciliation, and real-time inventory control. Although SWMX's share of TV and radio ads is small, it is growing fast, having booked $7 million in ad buys in the fourth quarter of 2006, which was a 52 percent increase over the third quarter of that same year. (Source: http://www.swmx.com/releases/27IRQ4TransactionVolume21507.pdf).

Bid4Spots (bidforspots.com) provides a similar service for advertisers seeking to advertise on both traditional radio stations and on one or more of the 25,000 online radio stations currently transmitting content. It uses a weekly, reverse auction in which stations compete for advertiser dollars. According to the company, through this auction advertisers realize savings of as much as 70 to 90 percent off the station's rate card. And given that such discounted spots would ordinarily not have been sold before, radio stations benefit as well. At the time this manuscript was being completed, Bid4Spots was in a partnership with eBay, which will certainly provide eBay with another opportunity to experiment with auction media while continuing to pursue the eBay Media Marketplace.

SpotRunner (spotrunner.com) provides both automated media planning and an automated solution to the actual mechanics of assembling a TV or radio spot from a library of prerecorded video modules, which can be customized by the advertiser. The total price of such a creative costs as little as $500. Once one has been assembled, a simple wizard-driven interface allows the advertiser to target this creative using geo- and demo-targeting. SpotRunner's approach to reducing creative production costs has earned it the interest of both CBS and WPP, which made significant equity investments in the company in 2006. (Source: Press release: http://72.14.209.104/search?q=cache:xiLqUTr63vsJ:www.spotrunner.com/pr/materials/PR_20061030.pdf+%22WPP%22+%22Spotrunner%22&hl=en&ct=clnk&cd=4&gl=us)

Visible World (visibleworld.com) and OpenTV (opentv.com) are entrants whose technology allows marketers to create customized advertising quickly, enhancing the relevance and value of television spots delivered through cable networks. By utilizing the granular, highly accurate information cable networks have about viewers in their subscription databases, marketers can create personalized ads precisely targeted toward their actual viewer households. Furthermore, based on the likelihood that an individual is watching a program within that household, they even target at an individual level. This technology also allows marketers to program advertising to respond to exogenous events, such as the instantaneous score in a sports event, or changes in the weather.

Other players in the race to replace untargeted broadcast ads with narrow-cast targeted advertising include Navic, Vyvx, and InVidi. Microsoft has expressed a strong interest in set-top box programming. It has a Media Center version of its Windows XP operating system, and all the Media Center functionality has been included in the Vista Ultimate upgrade. Microsoft's IPTV (also called Microsoft TV) is an operating system for set-top boxes that also runs on an Xbox 360 game console. With the integration of an IPTV platform and game console, Microsoft is in a position to make a play for control of the living room, including the advertising targeted at a household or consumer level. Microsoft's LiveID spans across the gaming, e-mail, and search and mobile platforms. In the meantime, Google is testing IP-addressable cable-TV advertising with Astound Broadband, a small cable TV provider.

Consequently, there is no shortage of innovation in the development of a next-generation advertising marketplace, but it's too early to tell which firm will deliver a winning system. But we can say the criteria for winning is dependant upon the developers of such a marketplace being able to deliver on several promises simultaneously:

- Critical mass: a large pool of advertisers to ensure the fairness of auction clearing prices
- A digitally enabled platform that assures that advertising assets can be delivered with minimal cost (no friction)
- A marketplace that is trusted and agrees that the media assets are authentic

For media owners looking to participate in the marketplaces, the challenge is in defining the intangible value that a particular publisher/broadcaster delivers in a way that still allows that inventory to be distributed through a marketplace. Direct media sales will likely continue for several generations, but there may be a profound shift over the next several years to marketplaces. All the foundational elements are in place.

Let's not confuse auction-based media with media networks. Media networks (both auction and nonauction) are in a constant conundrum. They want to grow, but the only publishers who want to join a network are the ones that have poorer-quality inventory than the network they want to join. This can be cured through transparency.

Many publishers and broadcasters, however, are not excited about the emergence of auction networks or discrete auction media marketplaces. They prefer the old-school sales methods, regardless that the commissions and transaction costs only add friction. If the industry doesn't like the auction-based media concept, and Google, eBay, Microsoft, or a heavily funded startup believes there are significant inefficiencies to be eliminated, those players are in a position to put their money where their mouth is. Google or other players, for example, could start by buying the media and then auctioning it off in an arbitrage model to prove its value. Once the value is proven, those with substantial captial and market cap can then go shopping for undervalued media companies.

CHAPTER 9

Conclusions

"A visionary is one who can find his way by moonlight, and see the dawn before the rest of the world."

—Oscar Wilde

✳

THE RAPID EVOLUTION of an entirely new advertising ecosystem requires an entirely new way of thinking about the way advertising works. Media planning and the advertising message (the "creative") are becoming inexorably linked, and therefore a successful marketing campaign must reflect this new complexity and dynamism. Creativity—the criterion by which successful advertising was gauged—will remain a central value, but this term will increasingly acquire a new meaning that will extend it beyond the creation of messaging to include the means by which these messages are delivered to multiple niche audiences. As new forms of digitally based media appear and morph, marketers will face rapid and unprecedented challenges to evaluate and exploit the marketing potential provided by each. Yet the same principles that have already been established in the marketplaces by the search engines will continue to apply, including that targeting and relevance create value for all participants in the ecosystem, that consumers will be increasingly empowered to choose their media, and that advertisers must create advertising that is *both* meaningful *and* relevant.

The forces behind the transformation of advertising have been building for a long time, driven by the increasing power of the consumer to choose which advertising to engage with or pay attention to. Marketers have long suspected that the broadcast media they buy is overpriced, the sample-based measurement tools used to assess the effectiveness of advertising are antiquated, and mainstream ad agencies and broadcasters are inadequately providing the accountable, multi-channel campaigns required in an era of fragmented and overlapping media consumption. DVRs and commercial-skipping behavior among the most valuable segments of the audience (high-income households) have exacerbated this situation. Couple this with the runaway success of new, automated forms of advertising pioneered by the major search engines, and there is a genuine crisis of confidence in the advertising establishment.

Institutional inertia, old-school attitudes, and a failure to embrace disruptive changes have all stifled the evolution of the institution known as Madison Avenue. Advocates of the status quo—and there are many—claim that television and other macro-targeted media will never go away, that marketers seeking scale will continue to buy tonnage to reach large audiences, and that Madison Avenue will adapt its practices to new media such as the Internet in the same way that it evolved its practices to handle the advent of television in the 1950s. Therefore, broadcasters and the networks similarly minimize the challenge ahead. Instead of embracing change, they have invented reasons to explain why it is impossible to bring automation, reduced friction, and market transparency to media buying. They cite that network buys are too complex to be auctioned on either a spot-by-spot or aggregated basis and bristle at the suggestion that what they do can be "commodified."

These broadcasters have a great deal to lose by reforming the way media is bought and sold, and they're not going to allow the change without resistance. They hope that by boycotting the future, they can make it yield. But the unmet needs of marketers to use more efficient ways of conducting their advertising and marketing operations are now being met by outside players, led by the search engines, that have devised methods, platforms, and metrics appropriate for reaching the divergent needs of consumers who are empowered by choice—consumer's choice in particular. These new platforms are powerful, yet they pose new problems for marketers, especially in managing the complexity that accompanies this power. Transparent media marketplaces are the wave of the future, and their efficacy has been demonstrated by Google and the other engines who are pioneering ways to make the pricing of advertising rational and its consumption relevant and nonintrusive. Those who would obstruct this evolution will learn a terrible lesson: consumers and marketers, not agencies and broadcast networks, have seized control of advertising's future.

While Madison Avenue fiddles, the Internet is burning with a fever of innovation whose pace continues to accelerate. The search engines themselves continue to expand their domain into nonsearch media such as radio, television, print, and others. New platforms such as YouTube, MySpace, and other contenders commanding millions of "eyes" rise unexpectedly, reach critical mass, are acquired, corporatized, and then are challenged by insurgent newcomers. Users tend to be inherently fickle, and they seek out the next coolest spot to hang out, watch and/or upload videos, chat, talk, and otherwise establish a virtual "nest." But these nests are temporary, and as soon as something better, faster, cheaper, or cooler comes along, these same users will be gone. At the same time, the lines between media owner (publisher/broadcaster), ad network, and ad agency are blurring. The CMO has the obligation to consolidate and understand all the information, and then move quickly to develop partnerships with the right diversity of vendors.

Change is constant, and its pace is accelerating continuously. There is no way to accurately predict the precise form that emergent digital ad marketplaces will take. What we can say, however, is that the same principles that are now evident—that targeting creates value, consumers will be increasingly empowered to choose their media, and advertisers will need to create meaningful and relevant advertising—will provide the foundations for these new marketplaces.

In order to succeed in this new world, marketers need to be fluent with technology, understanding both its potentialities and its limitations. They also need to be able to perform course corrections in mid-flight and be ready to take risks on emergent forms of media that are too new to have demonstrated their worth in the traditional sense. This means institutionalizing risk into your decision making in a way that's never before been necessary.

We're not talking about making decisions "by the gut" or "flying blind." Quite the opposite: success means staying very close to the market you're in, watching for developments that are just around the corner, and being able to quickly dominate opportunities before others do so. In other words, watch where the eyes, ears, and hearts of consumers are going, and then place savvy bets.

What we're describing is a world that's very different from the one we once knew. It is a much faster and uncertain world, where what's right today is wrong tomorrow, and where today's success is tomorrow's failure. Forward-thinking marketers will benefit from understanding and exploiting how rational advertising markets work, and forward-thinking agencies will adapt their practices to the radically altered marketing landscape. Operating in this environment is not for the faint of heart or the slow of feet, and not everybody is cut out for it. But for those who are willing to invest in the tools, techniques, and processes necessary to achieve mastery in this fast-moving world, there are many rewards. Those who can adapt will thrive, and those who can't or won't will wither and expire.

As marketers, we need to be aware that today's sure wager may be tomorrow's losing bet. We can't become complacent with any marketing medium because that medium is likely to disappear or, in a "tragedy of the commons" scenario, become overloaded with competing marketers in the blink of an eye. What we can do is watch what's happening closely, build nimble teams, and place our bets with our advertising dollar as sagaciously as possible, all the while knowing that our decisions are all provisional in a dynamic marketplace that grows more unstable every day. Still, the opportunities are so rich, and the potential so vast, that we gladly face the challenges of today's digital-marketing environment. Marketers who win in the digital media world, where "the eyes have it," are the same marketers who embrace change, respect the need for relevance in advertising messages, and constantly rethink their agency selections, technology requirements, and media and communications strategies.